Prison Journal

Prison Journal

Luise Rinser

translated by Michael Hulse

M
MACMILLAN
LONDON

First published in West Germany 1946 by S. Fischer Verlag
GmbH, Frankfurt am Main, under the title *Gefängnistagebuch*

This English translation first published in the United Kingdom 1987
by MACMILLAN LONDON LIMITED
4 Little Essex Street London WC2R 3LF
and Basingstoke

Associated companies in Auckland, Delhi, Dublin, Gaborone,
Hamburg, Harare, Hong Kong, Johannesburg, Kuala Lumpur,
Lagos, Manzini, Melbourne, Mexico City, Nairobi, New York,
Singapore and Tokyo

British Library Cataloguing in Publication Data

Rinser, Luise
  Prison journal.
  1. Prisons—Germany
  I. Title   II. Gefängnistagebuch. *English*
  365'.4'0924   HV9549

  ISBN 0-333-44968-1

Photoset by Rowland Phototypesetting Limited
Bury St Edmunds, Suffolk
Printed in Hong Kong

Introduction

On 12 October 1944, following a friend's denunciation, a young widowed writer and mother of two children was arrested at her home in Kirchanschöring, a village on the River Salzach in Bavaria, and taken to the women's prison at Traunstein to await her trial. The charge was high treason; the writer was Luise Rinser.

Luise Rinser had already attracted the disfavour of the Nazis, and since 1942 had been banned from publishing, and was under Gestapo surveillance. She had published her earliest story in the *Neue Rundschau* in 1938, at the age of twenty-seven, and in 1941 her first novel followed, *Die Gläsernen Ringe* [*The Glass Rings*], a sensuous account of the end of childhood in Catholic Bavaria. The lucid beauty of that novel won Luise Rinser the admiration of Hermann Hesse; but if its values were the values of the spirit, that was all the more reason for the Nazis to be suspicious of a writer who had already resigned her teaching job rather than yield to pressure to join the party.

The woman who was taken to Traunstein that October day was a woman of extraordinary character and sensitivity, and as we read her *Prison Journal* we are impressed by the striking mixture of strengths and frailties, knowledge and naivety. In her early thirties, Luise Rinser is a committed socialist, politically wide-awake and alert to the cross-currents of the times, and with a deep aversion to the attitudes that create societal hatred wherever she finds them: nationalistic humbug in a Frenchwoman is as repugnant to her as it is in a German. At the same time, Luise Rinser shows us clearly (and at times unwittingly) that her socialism, though deeply felt, is that of a woman whose life has been thoroughly bourgeois and, till the harsh war years, relatively sheltered: in the prisoner's responses we still sense childhood in a teacher's family, the regular visits to the venerable monastery of Wessobrunn, the proper steps in an ordered life (studies, engagement, teaching job, marriage). In part, the *Prison Journal* is the record of the unsentimental education of a woman brought up, often roughly, against other lives that have lacked her privileges, aspirations, and ideals.

The Luise Rinser we meet has considerable inner resources of curiosity, understanding, flexibility, and spiritual scrutiny. The spiritual scrutiny is rarely spelt out, and in her preface Luise Rinser remarks that she has 'made no mention whatever of the crisis in my wrestle with God,' but throughout we sense ourselves in the presence of a woman who remains firmly on the side of Life and Hope, and when on 7 November she writes, 'There is no stronger power than the spirit,' we pause to think how different this confrontation with evil is from Winston Smith's in Orwell's *1984*, where the horrifying point is precisely that the spirit is not strong enough to offer resistance indefinitely. Luise Rinser remains uncrushed. Her spirit emerges whole from her experience; her curiosity is rewarded with memorable observations; her understanding and human flexibility are greatly enriched. The process is not without its moments of temper, despair, and humour.

If we remember *1984*, and the many masterful works of prison literature, both factual and fictional, which our century has unfortunately produced, we see (as she is the first to admit) that Luise Rinser's prison confinement was by no means the worst conceivable. She was not physically tortured, she was not kept in solitary confinement, she was not subjected to brainwashing techniques. Luise Rinser is aware that elsewhere in Nazi Germany sufferings far more terrible were being endured, and she makes modest claims for her book. Yet as we read her *Prison Journal* any notion we might have of a graded scale of horror becomes palpably absurd and irrelevant. Any experience of prison starts with the fact of the loss of freedom, and in Luise Rinser's case, if the war had not been ended in time, that experience would have ended in a death sentence. Traunstein women's prison was not Auschwitz, but Rinser's too was a dark night of the soul, and what abides with us as readers is the powerful, bright image of a woman enduring that night, writing her notes on her scraps of paper, her hands chapped, her kidneys hurting, the other women in the cell weeping or ranting or bitching or making noise or stench, all her resilience movingly centred on her one existential act of writing.

The *Prison Journal* was one of the first books by a German writer to appear in post-war Germany (in 1946), and since then it has sold steadily and enjoys an undiminished reputation. With the novels and stories that Luise Rinser published in the 1940s and 1950s, it brought her the respect of Thomas Mann, Carl Zuckmayer, Oskar Kokoschka, Annette Kolb, Alma Mahler-Werfel, and others. As if her wartime experiences had given her a taste for discomfort, Luise Rinser has consistently chosen the thornier options, in her life and in her writings, and her diversity over the past four decades has been remarkable. In addition to a constant flow of novels and stories, she has written extensively on the Roman Catholic church (particularly on the reforms of Vatican II and the role of women in the church); she has written on the politics of West Germany, on literature and art, on feminism, on prison reform, on education; she has written diaries, travel books, plays, and children's books. All are marked by compassion and warmth, but also by an urgent attempt to write of even the most complex subjects in a straightforward way, an attempt that has led her supporters to bracket her with Heinrich Böll and her detractors to dismiss her. Her life has been rich in incident: marriage to the composer Carl Orff, work in a leper colony, vilification by a hysterical press which in 1977 labelled her a terrorist sympathiser, nomination by the Greens for the office of Federal President in 1984. Through it all, firmly and with humour and warmth, she has remained her own woman.

There is no easy approach to so many-sided a writer. But at the heart of Luise Rinser's work and vision, today as in the 1940s, there is compassion, abhorrence of violence, and love of her fellow human beings. These qualities make the *Prison Journal*, for all its occasional darkness, a sustaining and life-enhancing book.

Michael Hulse

Preface

One year after the end of the Second World War I published my prison notes in book form. This *Prison Journal* was one of the first German books to appear after the war. It sold out quickly. After the second impression I didn't want any more, for several reasons. The first: in the mean time I had heard so much about the suffering of those who were in concentration camps that my own experiences no longer seemed worth mentioning.

The second: in 1947 the 'Special Ministry for De-Nazification' in Württemberg invited me to lecture to several hundred SS internees at Ludwigsburg camp near Stuttgart. Ventures of this kind were termed 're-education'. I spoke on a highly relevant and highly problematic subject: 'Towards an Analysis of the Post-war German', and naturally it dealt with what was then very recent history. I was quite alone with the internees, who were without exception intellectuals: scholars in various fields, journalists, high-ranking bureaucrats. I don't know what gave me the courage to go ahead. Suffice to say I had that courage. About halfway through my lecture, a small group left the room, in tight military formation. Most remained. There was to be a discussion at the end. There was no discussion, but instead confessions of a shattering kind. I could see and feel that many of them were prepared to admit their mistakes and guilt, to learn anew, and to take their places in the work of reconstruction, no matter in what position. Afterwards I tried to secure the release of these men. The government of the day missed an opportunity. For years I received letters from several of these people, and in the end they sank back into their old world, resigned. (Today, it is true, some of them have been wholly integrated, but they no longer remember their past at all – that is what I mean by the missed opportunity of 1947.) But at that time I said to myself, as I pondered the new impression of my prison journal, that it was better to put an end to bitter contemplation of the past, and merely to want the future.

My third reason: I no longer liked the book at all. It struck me as hard and cold, and thus falsified my experience of imprisonment. My experience had been greater and profounder and filled with far more passion. But during my captivity I had very little paper, none at all in the end, and I had very little time in which to write, I simply wrote brief notes cued to keywords and wrote down facts. I said little or nothing about a good deal of what went on within me, such as the discovery of a quite new, realistic love of man as he is and not as he ought to be or as I wanted to see him; it was only in the most degraded of people that I got to know and love mankind at all. And furthermore I made no mention whatever of the crisis in my wrestle with God, who permitted all this misery and seemed unreachably far away; but this struggle happened so deep inside me that I was unable to write about it. When I shaped the notes into a book in autumn 1945, I kept very close to them, for I wanted nothing but a totally true, photographically exact image of life in a prison, and not a confession of my inner, subjective experiences. Later I regretted not having written about them, but I was uninclined to add anything. But now the book displeased me for that very reason, and so I wanted to let it disappear without comment.

Today, nearly two decades later, two of the reasons I have mentioned for not having a new impression no longer seem to apply, and indeed I have more reasons than I once did for wanting the book in print again.

At that time, in thinking one should let the dark past be, for the sake of the brighter future, I was making a mistake in my reasoning that many others made too. Today I know, as many others do too, that there is no such thing as a future that can be separated from the past and made independent. I even know that there is no such thing as the past. The past is locked into the present and is inseparably one with it. The present, and that other present we call the future, are nothing other than the fruit of our past. They sit in judgement on all that has gone before. For a while it is possible to imagine one is rid of all the past. But one day it appears before one and turns out to be a narrow defile through which (and no other way) the path to the future leads. If we flinch from the strait gate we never gain our freedom. We have to have the courage to examine our past, even if we do not like it, and it is then, at that precise moment when we recognise and admit how bad it was, that the door to a better future opens. It is for the sake of that future that this book, and all those books that revive our awareness of the dark past, should be read.

As far as my own displeasure in the book is concerned, I have to say that that is unimportant. Nor is it of any importance that many of my readers will be disappointed and shaken by the image of myself which they will come upon here from an unaccustomed angle. But they should realise that this was the first time I saw myself in this way, so nakedly, and that what I saw was predominantly what I found new and strange in myself, and that was what I wrote down. The rest I took and still take for granted.

The final and decisive stimulus for this new impression was given me a few months ago, to be exact on 18 January 1963, in the station waiting room at Hamm in Westphalia and then in the train from Hamm to Braunschweig. The train was running an hour late and those connecting with it went to sit in the waiting room. A tall, powerful man sat down without asking at the same table as myself – he was my age and presently started up a particularly sensitive conversation. The young people of today, he said, were bad and had no ideals, and in his day everything was different. He had joined the SS early on and 'stuck with it heart and soul right to the very end'. And his ideals? They were all a young man needs: belief in the future of his own *Volk*, loyalty, discipline, and keeping his nose clean. I asked what he meant by keeping his nose clean. Not chasing skirts, he said, and no excesses, and discipline. I put an unambiguous question to him: 'Did keeping your nose clean involve murder too?' Murder? They didn't commit murder! They did their duty as soldiers just as any other man did in time of war. I reminded him of the concentration camps. The question vexed him. The people in the camps were only criminals and enemies of the state, he said. And what about the Jews? They were enemies of the state as well. And Jewish women, Jewish children? All that was propaganda and rumours put about by the Americans – he himself could testify how rumours like that came into existence: when the bodies were dug out after the Dresden bombing they were filmed, and later the Americans used the footage claiming it showed concentration-camp victims. Finally I asked him

4

if he never had the feeling he had done anything wrong. No, he cried out, and if I had my time over again I'd do everything exactly the same.

Of course I know that nobody nowadays reveals his dubious past unless it causes him distress of some kind. If he does so it is because he feels the urge to confess – or to provoke, which amounts to the same thing, a wish to understand the past and political and personal failure. In this sense that conversation had a positive side, but I did not understand that till much later. For the moment, the encounter had got me so worked up that I couldn't help talking about it in the train when a fellow traveller wondered how I could live in Italy among a people that had no ideals other than money and where the young people were so corrupt ... There were already four other people in the compartment. I shall have to ask the reader to believe me when I say that the following scene happened exactly as I describe it. These four travellers were: an elderly woman who had the look of a Czech Jewess, a man from Dresden, a well-fed and bejewelled woman from the Rhineland, and a protestant minister who was reading the novel *The Last of the Just* by the Jewish author André Schwarz-Bart. When I recounted my brush with the SS man, the Czech woman immersed herself in her newspaper, deliberately paying no attention. The man from East Germany shrugged his shoulders and said that in the east they had other, more serious problems than the gabbling of one SS man (and that is true enough). The woman from the Rhine shouted out: 'Those poor SS men, they were forced to join, they were fine strapping lads. But why talk about politics? I've never bothered with politics.' 'Haven't you?' I asked. 'Never? Not even in 1933?' 'No, not then either!' 'And then', I said, 'we got

Hitler.' She gave me a stupid look. 'As if I could have done anything about that!' she said. I turned to the minister, seeking support. 'You know,' he said rather nervously, 'it's all so complicated. It depends which way you look at history.' 'And which way,' I asked, 'was the past good?' He was silent. So was I. We were all silent.

It is because of that silence that I have decided to allow this book to appear again after all. We have heard many voices in the past decade, many consciences have been awakened, and there have been many attempts at atonement. We must not allow what has been awakened to slip back into sleep. Only when we have fully 'seen' our past, whether we committed the crimes or were victims of them, will we have a future. This book is intended to assist that endeavour.

For the reader who will quite rightly be curious I should like to add what was not recorded in the book at that time. While I was in detention, I was being tried at the *Volksgerichtshof** in Berlin, under the notorious Freisler.† The charge was high treason (sedition, and resistance to the Third Reich). I was tried in my absence since they either couldn't or wouldn't transport me to Berlin in the final months of the war. I was not needed there anyway. Even

---

* The *Volksgerichtshof*, or People's Court, was established in April 1934, when the acquittal of three of the four accused in the Reichstag fire trial left Hitler dissatisfied with the *Reichsgericht* (Supreme Court). The People's Court existed to try treason cases, and was presided over by seven judges, five of whom were from the Nazi party, SS or armed forces. Its sessions were held in camera and there was no appeal against its verdicts. (Translator)

† Roland Freisler was the president of the People's Court, 'a vile, vituperative maniac' (William Shirer). His brutal, ranting behaviour in court was notorious; a newsreel of his conduct as judge was shown during the war crimes trial in Nuremberg. He was killed by an American bomb on 3 February 1945. (Translator)

without my being present I could be sentenced to death on the basis of the available documents. Things looked black for me. How I came to be saved was something I did not find out until some time after the war. When my lawyer, Dr Merkenschlager of Traunstein, asked me if I didn't know any prominent Nazi who could put in a good word for me, I was stumped at first (whoever did I know!) but, after long thought, came up with Professor Karl Ritter, the UFA* film director. I knew he was one of the oldest party members and a friend of Goebbels. He in turn knew that I was an opponent of the regime, but we got on well. When he was informed of my arrest he immediately approached Goebbels and assured him that the arrest was a mistake, that he knew me, and that the denunciation was a lie. Goebbels had my files sent to him by the Gestapo in Munich. Several weeks passed. But Goebbels could not simply allow my files to disappear, as the Gestapo and the Reich security services were already too familiar with my case. So in the end Goebbels had to return the files to Munich, but with the proviso that my case should be investigated anew. This re-examination took place. Ritter heard about it and intervened a second time, taking a great risk in doing so. Once more the files were sent to Berlin. And this time they stayed there. For Berlin was burning, the war was over, I was free. And so I owe my life to Karl Ritter, bearer of the party's gold medal, and I do not want to gloss over that fact here. What this man did was a remarkably decent act, and it was not an isolated case. It was not all as simple as foreigners sometimes suppose – that all Nazis were villains and all their victims

* The *Universal-Film-Aktiengesellschaft*, or Universal Film Company. (Translator)

heroes and martyrs. Things are not so easy, and it is good that they are not.

But what became of my friend who denounced me, and what of her husband in the 'active Gestapo'? My friend took over her husband's job while he was interned after the war. He was a schoolteacher. Now he is a schoolteacher again, and has been for a long time. And thus a murderer (for what else was he? – deliberately handing me over to the hangman) is educating children. I wonder: did he undergo such a change in the few years after the war that children can be entrusted to him? Perhaps it was wrong of me not to prevent him getting his job, by intervening with the Bavarian state government. I don't know. It is as I wrote to my friend in my reply after the war: I have left God to do the judging, because I for my part do not want to add a single link to the chain of revenge. Let us all have the chance to atone and to grow honest.

Luise Rinser, 1963

Foreword to the First Edition

I am publishing my prison journal. I am not doing this because my personal fate seems important to me. It is merely one among many thousands. But because it is one among thousands it is possible for me to publish this book. It does not speak of anything extraordinary, anything that might match the sufferings of those who were in the concentration camps. It is no more than everyday life in a prison for detainees in the Third Reich. What I report here is fact, not literature. It can be attested by everyone who lived through those months with me.

There are many who now say that these terrible, sad events should be laid to rest and forgotten. Many who, like myself, were able to escape the hangman or the camp only because the Third Reich collapsed, were broken by their experiences. They would rather hear nothing more about it. Some say it is dangerous to make the living look again into the depths of evil. And some feel it is too cheap to publish personal experiences of this kind. I have considered all of these objections. And I think they are wrong.

It is understandable that many do not want to hear any more about things they themselves experienced. It is not for them that this book was written. It is for those who saw and experienced none of it, who suffered hardly or not at all beneath fiendish ways of destroying man's freedom; it is for those who do not want to grasp that everything nationalism and militarism strove after by means of force today leads straight to total destruction; and it is for those who remain snug in a bourgeois security that is almost unscathed and have never learnt the truth of that bitter line in Brecht's *Threepenny Opera*: 'We'd like to be good rather than rough. But things are not like that.' Those who say it is dangerous to show the depths of evil should remember that it is far more dangerous to keep silence about the truth and escape into a world of 'aesthetic intellectuality' to which memories of the crimes of evil are not admitted. Everything that is forcefully banished from the memory of mankind will return one day with fearful power to make its claims. For this reason I believe that we can overcome evil now only if, like incorruptible diagnosticians, we look at it from a hundred sides, and consider it, and apply the correct and thorough treatment in good time.

I cannot contradict those who tell me that what I have to report is too insignificant. I can only point out to them that I was not concerned with myself but with preserving the cruelty of prison life and thus the suffering of thousands.

I have often been asked if the months I spent in detention, waiting to be sentenced, were bad. Naturally they were bad for a human being to whom freedom is as important as the air she breathes. But I would not strike that period of torment out of my life. That time in prison was the turning point in my life. During those dark months I was nothing but a suffering human being, in danger, having to learn to confront the greatest jeopardy calmly, with no cover and without the illusions of

bourgeois life. Today, when people who have been delivered from such danger meet they realise with a shock that
they have become different people: 'Newly formed and
free and independent of fate.'

Luise Rinser

22 October 1944

Ten days in prison now. Sunday. I'd say it's five o'clock. I no longer have a watch. When I was brought here they took everything away from me except a comb, toothbrush, towel, and the dress I am wearing. For the last five minutes I've also had a pencil and a few sheets of paper. Under a loose floorboard I discovered some paper, a pencil, a candle-end, matches, and half a cigarette. The cigarette totally disintegrated, the paper is yellow with age; presumably it has been there a long time. It must be a safe hiding-place. I shall use it to conceal a diary I want to keep. Writing is strictly prohibited. I am writing nonetheless. When I was still free and could write when I wanted and as often as I wanted, I often doubted the point of the exercise; now I consider it a great personal good. The Word mercifully cushions me, coming between me and the naked experience of imprisonment.

Ten minutes later. The wardress's keys jingled. The flap on my cell door was pulled open. I leapt to my feet, filled with that absurd hope for sudden release that lives on in every prisoner, even if he has already been condemned to death. Somebody murmured: 'Political,' and the flap was slapped shut again and chained to. I paced up

13

and down the cell. It is ten paces long and four paces wide, very high and bare. A plank bed, hard and narrow, with a woollen blanket, a folding table, a collapsable bench, a wall fitting with a tin washbowl, a broken mirror, and the latrine bucket in the corner – that is all. The bucket is one of the worst evils of the prison. It stinks. It stinks with a repellent pungency of the chlorine that is sprinkled in it every morning. The lid won't close. At one time the walls of the cell were whitewashed. In the corners there are splashmarks of brown filth. Halfway up the surfaces are covered with the marks of dirty hands and writing and drawings, some of which are done in pencil or red crayon, though most are scratched in with the tin spoon. I find a good many Polish and French names. One Henriette Periolet wrote 'Vive la France' over a dozen times. Hatred of the country that robbed her of her freedom may have given her strength in her loneliness. A poem has been written in Polish under the window and I am sorry I cannot read it. A giant portrait, the head of a handsome man, has been done in red crayon, and written below it, 'I'll be faithful to you!' There is no shortage of comforting rhymes, such as,

> The bad times will be over soon,
> no matter what they do.
> Then we'll be rid of Hitler
> and all his party too.

Or: 'Don't cry, everything comes to an end, sooner or later. I was here five weeks. Some day they'll let you out too.' Written in a small hand, in a corner, are these moving words: 'Dear God, set me free soon. I am innocent!' Next to them: 'These lousy swine.' Above the bed there are countless 'calendars', with a line scratched in for each day spent here. In one I count thirty days, in another fifty and more. Some time or other everybody has a last day. I try to draw comfort from this for myself. Drawings predominate, without exception obscene pictures by various hands: the act of love in every aspect, with every detail, naive and over-explicit. Sexual fantasy clearly cannot even be dulled by the excessive quantities of bromine that make our weak morning coffee froth and leave it tepid and practically undrinkable. I am astonished that any desire can be felt here other than the desire for freedom.

It is getting dark. The window is high up, thickly barred, with panes of ribbed, frosted glass that you can see nothing through. Now supper is on the way, I can hear clattering. Then the long prison night begins, without any light (there are no light switches in our cells and we are not provided with any light, not even to eat or undress by), without a book, without a word from a fellow human being. Six o'clock is striking, I think.

23 October 1944

I have looked forward to this moment all day. Viewed from the morning, days here seem endless; but once the early forenoon has been got through, the hours pass relatively quickly. All I have to do is grow accustomed to being a prisoner every morning anew. The rest of the time I spend as if my mind had been scoured totally blank. The day begins at five o'clock with a frightful to-do in the lower two storeys. The male prisoners are woken earlier than we are. They drag their buckets out of the cells with a clatter, carry them to the washroom, and empty them out there.

Then their footfall recedes, clattering, dragging. It is silent again for half an hour. I lie awake. In this half hour I am fully alert; I am aware with a full clarity that I no longer have any freedom whatsoever, that I am behind a thick oak door which is closed with iron chains, bolts, and a massive lock, that I cannot get up and leave, that I cannot go to my children, that my life is threatened by dangers I have never yet faced and cannot control. I do not know what they are going to do to me. Every day I hope for a hearing before the examining magistrate. To-day my lawyer was here. He said the files on me had been sent to the Gestapo in Munich and could be here in about a week's time. To my questions he gave hesitant, evasive replies and vague words of comfort. My caution is such that even with him I repeat the same statements I made to the police during my first interrogation, every word of which I have imprinted exactly on my mind. My lawyer is a degree or so less cautious. Clearly he is a fierce opponent of the Nazis, but he is timorous and, naturally, his hands are tied. He seems to be one of the old liberals. Whether or not he sees through me completely I can't say. I have the definite feeling that he is utterly powerless before the Gestapo and that in political cases lawyers do their job only for the sake of appearances. I am pretty pessimistic about my own case.—I am tired. From seven in the morning till five in the evening I work in the sewing cell with two older women, who reacted to me with mistrust and silence at first, but are now already becoming a lot more talkative. They are both Jehovah's Witnesses; one of them, Frau M., is in here for the second time already, this time round it's been thirteen months so far, and the other woman has been here for eleven months. The fact that they are Jehovah's Witnesses is all that's needed for a charge of high treason. Jehovah's Witnesses are pacifist on principle; their husbands and sons are conscientious objectors. The son of one Jehovah's Witness, Frau W., was executed for this. His mother, who is in prison here, bears it without complaint. In all there are fifteen Jehovah's Witnesses here, the oldest of them eighty-five years old. They are all very remarkable, wonderfully tranquil, brave, strong in their faith, and acutely aware of their duties. They darn, patch, and sew prison laundry, and do it as well as if they were being paid for their work. What is more, they are well-nigh immune to the hardships of confinement, since for all of them it is a matter of certainty that one day 'perpetual peace' will dawn, not the peace of 'Heaven' but peace on earth. Then the Kingdom of Justice will commence; but first there will be a terrible battle in 'Armageddon', and the unjust who are in power on earth will be destroyed. They say the Nazis know all this, and that is why the Gestapo judges are so enraged if you fling a reminder of 'Armageddon' at them during a hearing. I object that it is too cosy to expect the healing of the body politic by forces beyond the human – we have to see to it ourselves (I say), which is why we have socialism. I try to make clear to them the basic principles of socialism. They shake their heads in a superior fashion; that's all nonsense, they say, only the 'Lord' will save us. They are confirmed in an impenetrable fanaticism. I do not feel any the wiser for all their dogma. It seems that apart from hatred of power and hope for Christ they have no ideas. I can place no trust in this doctrine, seeing how loveless its adherents are. For example, I observe that Frau W. has received a parcel from her relatives, which she hides fearfully in a corner, now and then nibbling a little, without giving so much as a scrap to any of us.—Or at lunch: through an oversight one bowl of food too many was brought to our cell. Frau P., being the eldest, does the sharing-out. They've cooked up something with potatoes and carrots. She fishes out the carrots for herself, and the sauce too, and leaves the potatoes for the rest of us.

24 October 1944

Last night I dreamt I was taken up onto a high mountain. I was shown Turkey: a large brown cloth, frayed, with a good many holes in the middle. I was to patch it up, but I refused on account of the Allies, who would consider it an intrusion on their rights. A nightmare! I have quite enough darning and stitching with the socks and thick prison bed-linen that is thrown into our cell in big heaps, often still damp. The laundry of the roughly 200 men and 150 women in our prison, and on top of that the laundry from the all-male detention centre at Bernau. There's scarcely an intact item in the lot, and often we've no notion how to patch them together again. We have no darning wool, and to mend the undergarments we have to use sewing cotton, likewise for darning socks. Our needles are far too thick, our scissors blunt, our wool tears at every stitch so that mostly, rather than darn the holes, all we do is cover them with thick patches of material. These harsh socks often scour the prisoners' feet in their heavy wooden clogs so raw that they simply tear off the patches, preferring to walk with holes in the soles of their socks. Recently we got some cast-off soldiers' uniforms, and were expected to sew women's skirts from them. One more year of this war and the prisoners will literally have only rags to cover

18

their bodies. Needless to say the prisoners wouldn't dream of looking after their clothing, they tear open the seams and lining to use them as hiding-places for things that have been smuggled in. At times we get garments that have obviously been torn to shreds senselessly, out of rage. Curiously, the dresses are all too long and above all far too big. The women and the young girls who still feel a need to look pleasing even in here usually shorten their skirts by simply tearing or cutting off a strip, make new buttonholes in the material with their fingers, or indeed even sew new seams with a few coarse stitches. Since they have nothing to sew with in the cells (knives, scissors, and needles are forbidden because of the suicide risk), and since they only rarely have any opportunity to steal, they pull the threads out of their old woollen blankets. Also, our bed-linen is only changed once a fortnight.

Today Frau M. and Frau P. told me about their arrest. The Jehovah's Witnesses were persecuted from the very beginning of the Third Reich, but a year ago a big wave of arrests passed over the whole of Germany and every last Jehovah's Witness was captured. They were interrogated in their home towns, and since the last thing they would do was deny their beliefs they were transported to the Gestapo in Munich in long, harrowing journeys. Frau P. said it was night when their transport train arrived there. They and their comrades were taken to a completely dark room, shoved in, and locked away. In the darkness they stumbled over things they took for sacks till they noticed they were people lying on the bare floor. There were hundreds of them. Without food, without blankets, without water they had been herded in here, men and women. During the night one old woman died of exhaustion. The corpse remained where it lay until morning. The people spent several days in this room. Bread and watery soup were all they were given to eat. For hundreds of people there were only four or five buckets. Women and men had to relieve themselves openly in front of each other; but there was not a single one among them who complained. After a few days they were interrogated individually. Frau P., when the Gestapo judge asked her, 'You are an opponent of Adolf Hitler, are you not?' replied, 'Yes, I am! Hitler is a tyrant, he is the Anti-Christ, he is an evil demon. But his time will soon be over. God Himself will topple him. Armageddon is nigh.' The judge leapt to his feet, kicked her in the stomach with his booted foot, and screamed the wildest curses. She, however, said calmly, pointing to the swastika: 'You are wearing the sign of the Anti-Christ. You will be destroyed along with it, but we shall live with Christ and help raise on high the kingdom of the just.' At this she was led away by an SS man, who pushed her with his fists and the butt of his rifle. Frau P. told us her only son was a conscientious objector and spent a year in prison but then he was released and stuck in the army. As his religion prohibits suicide, he was left no alternative but to go to war. But, Frau P. told us full of pride, he will not kill a single human being. The Gestapo drove the Jehovah's Witnesses through the whole town in open trucks, to needle them, and at length took them to Stadelheim prison near Munich. They report all this without complaint. To them it is understood that they suffer for their doctrine. 'In the Bible it is written': almost everything they say starts like this. 'It is written in the Bible that the just must suffer.' Even without referring to the Bible I have to concede their point.

25 October 1944

My lawyer has just been here. He said K.* had been to see him today, wanting permission to visit me, but he was turned away. He will not be allowed to see me until I have had my hearing. K. was here, here in this building, and I did not know it.

26 October 1944

These are bad days. Frau L., the youngest of our warders, who occasionally shows a trace of human sympathy for us, just told us Rosenheim has been bombed. My eldest son is staying there, with my parents – perhaps he is dead. Also I had a confrontation with the head wardress. She came into the sewing cell and shouted: 'You swine, see to it that you get to your cell and clean it up, I tell you it looks like a pigsty. I'd like to see how your own home looks! A swine like you!' The anger surged to my head, but I controlled myself. 'In the first place,' I said, 'I am not a swine, and you certainly don't have the right to call me one.' Frau M. made anxious gestures to me to be quiet, but that was impossible. 'In the second, my cell is tidy. If the floor isn't clean enough, give me a rag and a scrubbing brush – unfortunately I can't clean without them.' The wardress flushed crimson. 'You cheeky so-and-so,' she screamed, 'how dare a hussy like you contradict me!!' I jumped up: 'I won't be talked to like that!' She plunged at me and raised her hand to strike me. I did the same, and, still controlling

---

* Not Karl Ritter, but Klaus Herrmann, a homosexual writer from Berlin. Luise Rinser's husband, Horst Günther Schnell, had been killed on the Russian front in 1943. (Translator)

myself with an effort, cried out, 'You'd better not.' The tone of my voice, or something or other, made her feel she would be well advised to lower her hand and go. Frau M., pale with fright, said: 'Whatever have you done? She will notify the prison governor of your conduct!' Suddenly I was seized with fury. I hammered on the table and exclaimed: 'This female, this stupid sow of a woman with a swastika, who is she to abuse me? Are we still human beings in here?' 'For God's sake,' said Frau P., 'be quiet, this will be bad for us all. Have you only just realised that we have no rights?' To cap it all, a woman has been put in the next cell who sobs and weeps ceaselessly. She seems to be a Pole; she cries out incomprehensible sentences, at times inarticulately. This bottomless despair gets on my nerves.

27 October 1944

The Polish woman in the next cell, quite a young creature, was arrested for being an accomplice to theft. Her lover and his friend, two Polish workers, asked her to borrow bicycles from the farmers she worked for, just for the Sunday. Seemingly they took off homeward with them, and the farmer informed the police of the theft. Lioba, or whatever her name is, was put in gaol. The poor thing is in total despair here. Her lover left her in the lurch and, on top of it, thoughtlessly landed her in such a dreadful situation. That she knew nothing of their intention seems quite plain to me. Toward morning her agony peaked. She battered at the walls and doors with her head and hands and bawled. None of the warders came. I didn't sleep a minute. What is more I am beginning to feel hunger. For the first few days after I was brought here I ate nothing, partly out of defiance, partly rage, partly I was revolted by the rusty tin spoon and the battered tin bowls the food is brought in. But then I told myself it was pointless going hungry. No one was paying any attention to my passive resistance. Almost all the prisoners try a hunger strike at the outset, instinctively or from calculation, Frau P. told me, but they all give it up one day. There is little of the food, and it is poor stuff. There is a one-week menu that is constantly repeated, so you can predict months ahead what there will be to eat on (say) 5 January.

Sunday: a kind of goulash with potatoes cooked into it. From time to time you find a thread of meat or a lump of gristle. The juniper berries that float in it are rated a delicacy among us. They are the only seasoning the kitchen uses. In the evening there are two small pieces of bread, a small pat of margarine, and a spoonful of jam, and with it a little fruit tea.

Monday: sauerkraut, potatoes, in the evening a few potatoes in their jackets with cheap cheese. Usually half of the potatoes are bad, at times they are still hard.

Tuesday: potatoes cooked together with a few carrots; in the evening watery soup with bread.

Wednesday: a kind of hash, like Sunday's, with one or two scraps of meat and potatoes cut in slices; in the evening watery soup and bread.

Thursday: white cabbage with potatoes; in the evening watery soup and bread.

Friday: barley broth, a tiny piece of bad sausage (horsemeat sausage, they say); in the evening watery soup with bread.

Saturday: fried potatoes (fried in water, of course), and

a watery soup with them; in the evening, bread with a slice of cheap wurst.

All of this sounds quite passable, but it is only half-done, cold, unseasoned, with no fat, too salty or completely unsalted, unappetising, doled out in bowls that at times have scarcely been washed, and then on top of it all the tin spoon which you have to wash yourself in cold water with neither a dish-clout nor detergent. Sometimes you cannot get a meal down no matter how great your hunger. The food is by no means adequate. The complete absence of fat and sugar tells. I am rapidly losing weight. My clothes hang loose on my body, my face looks sunken and old; I've been finding grey hairs at my temples. I am starving. Frau M. told me I could have a package sent from home. Every week a pound of rye bread, a pound of white bread, a pound of fruit and a little jam are permitted. Everything else is prohibited. Every fourteen days I may write home. I shall ask them to send me food. I have to get through this at all costs.

28 October 1944

Still no hearing. Today Frau M. gave me half of her bread ration as she had received a parcel. The bread is already quite old and dry; so much the better. I save it up for the night. Mostly I wake up shortly before midnight and cannot get back to sleep for hunger. Today a new prisoner joined us in our sewing cell, a tall blonde woman, far gone in a pregnancy, in her eighth month. She was the lover of a Frenchman who came to Germany in 1940 as a prisoner of war but after the armistice with France was no longer treated as a prisoner here. It was by no means forbidden to have contact with Frenchmen who had been set at liberty. Frau H., whose husband has been missing for years, fell in love with Lucien, who, she told us, owns a chocolate factory in Paris and promised to marry her. She became pregnant by him. When this happened he promptly went to the mayor of the town and said the expected child was his. All well and good. But now that the French were fighting with the Allies against Germany, the French who were interned here were suddenly being treated as prisoners of war again. It had become a crime for a German woman to have a relationship with the 'enemy'. So Frau H. was taken to prison in spite of her condition. She sits there crying. Her pretty, pale face is thickly swollen. She does not eat, doesn't sew, stares ahead of her, and occasionally whispers her lover's name.

Today a prisoner who does work outside smuggled a newspaper in to us. In it there's a map of the Dutch theatre of war, and despite all the clever bamboozlement it's amply clear that the war is lost. Since yesterday wild rumours have been reaching us too. The Russians are said to be marching on Vienna. We grab at such news with both hands, for us it means liberation. But I distrust rumours. The war can still go on for months. This morning between eleven and half past I was out in the open again for the first time, that is to say, in the cramped courtyard between high stone walls. In point of fact we ought to get out in the fresh air for half an hour every day, according to the prison regulations. But the warders do not take the time out for this. Yesterday Frau L., a sub-warder, was in our sewing cell. She often brings us her stockings and underwear to mend and her dresses to iron. This isn't strictly speaking allowed, true, but the warders can do what they please. She chatted to us in her disagreeable way, a mixture of crude, gossipy sucking-up and laying her got-up claim to authority. She is indescribably stupid. We saw the sun was shining and at length Frau P. observed shyly that it was the weather for a walk in the courtyard. Frau L. exclaimed: 'God almighty, I was supposed to let you lot out! But it's too late now, it's practically half-past eleven and it's not worth it any more.' In that way we were done out of the day, of the bit of fresh air we so urgently need. Our faces are grey and slack. Today the head wardress herself was on duty. She does her duty drily and wickedly, with the correctness of a clock. She let us into the yard punctually, on the dot of eleven. We had to get in line in silence and wait before the barred gateway that closes our floor off from the stairs. For the first time I saw faces other than those of Frau M. and Frau P. As I have an insatiable curiosity to get to know people and their fates, I succeeded in learning a good deal in a short time, from secretly whispered sentences. In front of me went the bewitchingly lovely Frau N. She, like Frau H., was arrested on account of an affair with a Frenchman. Behind me, a short, hunchbacked woman with kindly eyes, a Jehovah's Witness. She has already been in gaol fourteen months and seems to be ill. Three young girls had a confrontation with the head wardress. They said they could not walk any more in their wooden clogs and showed her their ankles, chafed raw. They wanted to walk barefoot. The head wardress screamed that this was contrary to prison regulations and they had best go fetch their clogs. The girls refused. The head wardress gave each of them a resounding blow on the ear; she did it so quickly that they were unable to defend themselves. The youngest, only eighteen, declared she would complain to the public prosecutor of mistreatment

26

of prisoners – it wasn't allowed. The other prisoners laughed out loud, whereupon we all of us had first to stand in silence for five minutes without moving, while the head wardress gave us her stare. I considered her face. It is not ugly nor even bad, it is simply dry, expressionless, dead. Even when she boxes ears, or is hard or cruel, it is not the product of wickedness but of her inflexible sense of duty. I saw her laugh, once, when a prisoner fell down the steps. That laugh, which was not a laugh of *Schadenfreude* but rather of crude amusement at the little scene, was disturbing. It betrayed all of the coarse desolation of this person, who is no longer a human being but only a machine for supervising. For a moment I felt pity for her. Suddenly she demanded, in her rasping voice, 'You, you there, what are you gaping at me for?' I said, 'I was just wondering whether you are ever capable of feeling anything.' She cast me a suspicious glance and muttered something I couldn't catch. Right after this she ordered us down the stairs. We have to walk very slowly, in silence, one after the other, and wait at each one of the four barred gates, even if they are not locked. But on this trip I still learnt a thing or two. The three young girls are munitions workers from the underground munitions factory at H. They had run away and were aiming to get across the Swiss border, as they had been forced into the work. God knows how they imagined they would pull it off. Naturally they were caught. In passing it turned out – but I discovered this only afterwards – that the two younger girls had done a good deal of thieving. One is nineteen years old and this is already her third spell inside. She does not feel at all unhappy in prison, and the seven months she now has to spend there do not depress her. She wears her hair in long curls and her cheeks are painted. She explained to me in eager whispers that she had made curlers out of paper and torn-off strips of bed-linen; the warder, she said, was forever taking them away from her, but she always made herself new ones. The colour on her cheeks is floor-stainer which she steals from the cleaning closet.

When I got out in the open, for the first time in weeks, I felt giddy. The sun was shining brightly and warm on half of the small yard, the other half lay in the shadow of the high walls. We had to walk round and round the cramped courtyard, exactly as I'd seen in Van Gogh's prison picture, one after the other, in silence, round and round in a circle, happy for half a minute in the warm, sunlit half, and then shivering in the damp shadow for the other half minute. After twenty minutes we were herded into the building again.

29 October 1944

Yesterday I wrote so long in the dark that today I could hardly see to sew. So I was almost pleased this morning when I was ordered into the kitchen to scrub vegetables with Frau H. A bare, clean kitchen with two immense cauldrons for the prisoners' food and a large stove for the officers' food. Four of us had to peel a massive tubful of potatoes for the next day. Our lunch was already bubbling away in one of the two pots. As always on a Sunday it was a thin brown broth with slices of potato, juniper berries, and scraps of meat. A large, robust girl was stirring it with a stick. In the officers' oven a pork roast was sizzling away, and on the table stood a bowl of endive salad. We breathed in the smell of the roast and hastily stole a few leaves of

28

salad, which we gobbled down without any dressing, the first fresh vegetable we'd had in weeks. The cook, a forty-year-old ill-tempered female, saw this and shouted angrily: 'What do you think you're up to? Stealing? A fine thing, that salad's for the officers, see you remember it, you thieving lot.' I imagined she was a warder and felt cowed. About five minutes later I saw her in one of the next rooms secretly wolfing pieces of meat the size of her hand. She had no idea that her reflection could be seen in the open kitchen window. Not long after she took the roast out of the oven and bore it past our covetous eyes from the kitchen. When she returned she had a plate with a large juicy piece of pork on it. She ate it up before our very eyes. Suddenly I became aware of the spiteful faces and the murmuring of the other prisoners beside me. However, before I could ask the reason Fräulein B., an assistant warder, a young, good-natured person who was in the wrong place here, came into the kitchen. She was carrying a plate of fruit and steamed yeast-dumplings, which she placed before the cook. 'There, this is for cooking us such a delicious roast.' The cook grinned, and the plate disappeared into the next room, whither the robust girl who'd stirred the broth and another girl also in a white apron soon adjourned too. Clearly the three of them were eating up the plateful. My stomach was in revolt, and my sense of justice even more so. What did it all mean? We prisoners had eaten two small pieces of rye bread early that morning with our poor, milkless barley-malt coffee. Now it was nearly half-past eleven and all we had in our stomachs was a few lettuce leaves. Now I discovered a remarkable fact. The cook, Frau A., whom I had thought a civilian, was a prisoner; she had been given three years for misappropriating food in her capacity as owner of a large hotel in R. where an NSV* children's home had been installed. I can still remember reading the newspaper report at the time. She let the children go hungry and sold off the food at extortionate prices. Why is she not in one of the big gaols? Why is she acting the warder? Why is she being given the best food? Why is she getting preferential treatment? Why does she eat up the pieces of meat that are meant for the prisoners? Why, as Frau P. told me, is she allowed to go home frequently, to check whether her enterprise, which is 'essential to the war effort', is still running smoothly? Why won't she let us eat the one or two leaves of salad we so urgently need? Why does she call us thieves? Why is no one here protesting about her? Frau P. enlightened me; the matter is so simple. A. supplies large quantities of food to the prison, in secret. Who for? Not for the prisoners, that's for certain! Why does she receive a parcel every week, which other prisoners are not allowed to do? Why is she allowed a newspaper? The other two girls are her accomplices. One of them is in for a year and a half, no one knows exactly why. She is the daughter of the mayor of one of the nearby towns. The other is a young businesswoman with a three-year sentence. She was forging food ration coupons in massive numbers. The three of them look very well, red-cheeked, fat, healthy, while we are pale, lean, and weak. They share a cell. In the mornings and evenings they have light, they have hot water to wash, every evening they take a pot of tea with them from the kitchen, and each of them takes a box of food: margarine, bread and pieces of sausage, stolen from the rations that were intended for us. The prison administration, the warders and all the prisoners know this, and

* *Nationalsozialistische-Volkswohlfahrt*, the Nazi social welfare organisation. (Translator)

no one does anything about it. I shall never learn how to grasp the fact of the world's badness, its stupidity and evil. Lunchtime brought a small compensation. When I returned to the sewing cell I saw a young creature who instantly fascinated me. She is a Frenchwoman, seventeen years old, from Amiens. I immediately got talking to her. Her father was a communist. When the Germans occupied Northern France they captured him, his wife, and Jeanette, their only daughter. The father was sent to Siegburg concentration camp, the mother has disappeared, and Jeanette, who was sentenced to two and a half years in prison – at that time she was not yet fifteen – has been moving from prison to prison since then. She knows all the big southern German prisons, she knows the ropes. Now she is to be released in a few days. She is very pale, but curiously very well groomed, as if she had only just been put inside. When I first set eyes on her I saw that, without pausing in her sewing, she was quietly weeping to herself. As I addressed her in her mother tongue she smiled at me through her tears. When she spoke, it was an experienced, tormented, disillusioned person speaking. We whispered together for a long time. I asked why she was crying if she was due to be released. Oh, she replied, it would only be a make-believe release. She would be moved from the prison to a camp for foreign women, and that was nothing but a different kind of prison. I gave her my home address, which, experienced and cautious as she was, she scratched into her comb in unreadable letters. K. is to give her some of my clothing as she will have nothing, nothing whatsoever, after her release. This conversation comforted me, for the young girl, in her matter-of-fact braveness, put me to shame in my despair.

This morning at four we had a major alarm. We had to dress in the dark. Our few personal effects and the blanket were rolled into a bundle and we were driven down to the ground floor. The prison has a large air-raid shelter too, but that is only for the officials. Though it is open to a handful of prisoners too. I saw A., the cook, and her two sidekicks, and Z., who helps out in the office and also has a three-and-a-half-year sentence, vanish into the officers' shelter. The rest of us sat on our blanket bundles, which we had thrown down on the dirty floor of the long corridor. The house door was open but we ourselves, left unsupervised, lay behind a large, barred gate which was locked. If a bomb were to fall here we would be lost, since no one would open the gate for us if the force of the explosion didn't do it. The mere sound of the alarm is enough for all the officers to lose their heads, run around senselessly, and roar out pointless and idiotic orders. We cowered tired and frozen on the flags. We sat in the dark; only from the other floor did a little light fall through the gate, and the iron bars sketched a black shadowy trellis over us. A good film scene. Not so good for us, having to endure it. I have a cough, cold, and pains in my kidneys. We have identification tags round our necks, with numbers, just in case. Perhaps I shall be found sometime lying blown apart somewhere, perhaps they'll identify me by my number then – I am number 150.

Once again I have found out the stories of some of the others. Two sisters from northern France, with Rubens figures: blonde, rosy, strong, blooming, and dragged off to Germany. They worked as assistants in a Munich hospital. When they realised that the western front was pushing closer and closer to the Rhine they upped and left one day, to head toward the front. Oddly, they set out not westward but east, ended up in Berchtesgaden (of all places), and were arrested there. They have already been inside for six weeks and do not know when they will be released. Hunger doesn't seem to be troubling them. They are only suffering from being separated – naturally they were not put in the same cell. Each is on her own. I say 'naturally' because everything that might mean even the slightest easing of our detention is conscientiously eradicated. The two of them sat contentedly, in a tight embrace, softly crooning French popular songs to themselves. The younger one is stupid and harmless, but the elder is clever to the point of cunning. I can tell from the alert movements of her eyes that she is incessantly the observer, and what she sees is registered within. She despises the Germans, she hates us, and makes no bones about the fact. Speaking to me she was polite enough. She has a good knowledge of French music. She has also read a good deal of German literature in French translation. Whenever the younger one, in friendly mood, tries to butter up some German or other, she is brought up sharply by the elder. The other five Frenchwomen and Belgians, incidentally, behave in the same way. One cheeky, snub-nosed Belgian woman is in gaol because she called her employers 'boches'. I asked her why she did that. 'Ach,' she said, 'that's what all of you are.' I stayed calm. 'Why are we all boches?' 'You have no manners, you are coarse and ugly and you're all Nazis.' When I told her that the reason I am here is precisely that I am not a Nazi, she scrutinised me from top to bottom with an expression of disbelief and distrust, and then moved uneasily away. What a jingoistic hatred has been instilled in these girls and in the peoples they belong to! All those paths of mutual understanding that were beaten, with such effort, since the last war, particularly between Germany and France – what were they all for? I was sitting beside a young woman who told me and the others, without the smallest reserve, a lot of political jokes, starting with the most harmless, right up to the extremely dangerous. She – Frau S. – said she had been arrested on account of a friendship with two Russians. Her father was Russian and the simple fact was that she felt a certain sympathy for the people. A curious person, small, soft, intelligent, inscrutable, crafty, and dangerous. I suspect there is more to this than meets the eye. She is awaiting trial.

One girl, twenty years old, is in for infanticide. They say it is the second child she has murdered. The girl, black-haired and black-eyed, is pretty. Her motive is incomprehensible. She had the last child by a farmer's son. He would not have married her, but he would have taken the child to his farm and paid her off. Everything was all right. When she gave birth to the child she was alone. She hit its head against the edge of the bed until the baby was dead. Why? I asked her. 'I don't know,' she said. And that seems to me to be the truth of it. Neither fear of punishment, nor financial worries, nor hatred of the child's father impelled her to it. True, she has no great mind, but she is fully responsible for her actions. The hearing is to take place in three days' time. We have a second infanticide too, who has already received her sentence: three and a half years in gaol. A coarse, red-headed servant girl, whose brutal hands, chafed raw from washing laundry, are unsettling. She had an affair with a Pole. His paternity remained a secret. The child was born. The farmer family she was living with wanted to keep the baby and bring it up. One

34

day she strangled or smothered the three-month-old. What can have driven her to it? An upsurge of senseless rage? Perhaps the child was crying too much. Suddenly she found it a nuisance. Man is capable of wild, dark actions. The punishment is steep, and the question remains open whether the girl will be made any better by the three and a half years she spends washing and stitching sacks in a half-darkened cellar. I shouldn't want to be a judge.

1 November 1944

All Souls.—Tonight there was a big stir. Suddenly alarm bells were ringing, and the telephone. Immediately afterwards I heard the tooting of cars driving off, and some time later shots were fired all around the town. I was trembling with excitement, thinking the Russians or the Allies had arrived. Soon after, the cars drove up again, doors were slammed, bars were clanged shut, silence. —In the morning I discovered that two Poles had tried to escape. One had got away but the other had been shot and recaptured. Since the morning I have been filled with the crazy thought of escaping too. I was sent with Frau P. and Frau M. to fetch laundry from the attic where it is dried. We were on our own. We climbed up on the heating pipes and looked out of the skylights. Far down below the town lay in the mist, far off were hills with yellow and red deciduous woods, beyond them the mountains, with snow on them already. I could smell freedom. Frau P. must have sensed what I was thinking because she hauled me down energetically and said: 'Sheer poison. Come on down. Back to work.' But when I was alone for a moment I

35

climbed up again. The gutter runs a few metres below the window. At the roof's edge there is the strong cable of the lightning conductor. It leads down the wall of the building to the courtyard. A tree sags deep over the yard wall. You could give it a try.—I know this is nonsense. But the plan obsesses me. Tonight I suddenly resented K. bitterly for not attempting to free me. For example, he could charter an aircraft, circle low over the courtyard when we are allowed out to walk, let down a rope that I could take hold of in an instant, and I'd be off. I laugh at myself, but it seems this really is quite simply a component in the 'prison psychosis' (an expression you hear quite often here). For example, if you are ill and go to the doctor: 'You aren't ill, it's just prison psychosis.' The phrase is familiar to even the least educated here.

This afternoon the alarm sounded again. For two hours we were sitting in the cold ground-floor hallway. We were already cowering in our places when the men who work outside returned. They passed us on their way to the cells. Suddenly Frau H., the one who is pregnant, cried out softly. She had recognised her Lucien among the prisoners. She had no opportunity to say anything to him. Now he too has been arrested.—Today Frau Sch. was on duty. She is a nervous, uncouth female. When we grew a little too loud she yelled: 'You bolshevists, you pack of commies, you Russians, I'll put you under detention if you don't shut your traps.' She is wholeheartedly detested. I was sitting next to the group of 'smiths', ten women who stamp iron in a munitions works. They are the most rebellious. They say Frau Sch., who supervises them when they work outside, beats them. Recently they had to push a wagonload of heavy iron bars up a slope. It was almost beyond their strength, and for a moment they paused. Promptly Frau Sch. leapt at them, struck out at their heads with the metal frame of her bag, and drove them on. Passers-by witnessed the incident and protested, but so far nothing has come of it. It would amaze me if anything did. Not long before the alarm was over a tall, lean man joined us. I assumed he was a new warder or some skilled worker, but he was the public prosecutor. In a tone that expressed the greatest unwillingness to talk to us, he rasped, 'Anyone who has wishes or complaints or applications to make, step forward.' Frau S., the eldest of the smiths, a resolute woman from Bremen, stood up and said: 'Are the warders permitted to beat us?' The public prosecutor pulled a sour face. 'How do you mean?' he asked sullenly. Frau S. went on courageously: 'Frau Sch. beats us. There are seven witnesses here.' The public prosecutor said dismissively: 'I know, I know. I heard.' Frau S. grimaced angrily and then added: 'Frau Sch. calls us bolshevists, communists and Russians. Is that permitted?' We laughed. The public prosecutor made a dismissive gesture and murmured, 'I haven't the time for trivial matters such as that. Go on. Next.' Frau H., the pregnant one, said: 'I'm eight months gone and in constant pain. I have asked to be allowed to see my doctor, but they are not letting me do so.' The public prosecutor: 'What do we have a prison doctor for? Go to see him. Next.' Frau H. called out: 'But I went to see him and he said there's nothing the matter with me, it's prison psychosis.' Frau S. put in: 'She's hungry, that's what's up. How can a woman far gone in a pregnancy live on watered soups and potatoes? Out there you get high-grade milk and butter – Hitler rewards you for bringing a child into the world, and here you have to starve for it.' 'Be quiet,' said the public prosecutor, bored, 'or I shall put you in detention.' 'Ach,' said Frau S., 'as if that'd make any difference in my case.' The public prosecutor affected not to hear this comment. 'Right, next,' he said. Another woman, tall, intelligent, said: 'When I was brought here I had a pound of butter in my bag. The butter is in the personal effects room. I have now been here fourteen days. I wanted to send the butter to my son in the field. It'll be going off. Can the kitchen melt it to lard and get it to him?' The public prosecutor yawned to show how greatly we were boring him. 'You can give the butter to someone to take home for you.' 'But who?' cried the woman angrily. 'That's impossible.' 'Fine, then we'll just have to use the butter in the kitchen here.' 'But my son needs it.' 'Hard luck, you're in prison now, aren't you? Next?' The tall intelligent woman said in an undertone: 'Another little proof of how right I was to complain to the *Reichsgericht*.'* The public prosecutor gave her a malicious but uncertain look. It seems something unusual is going on here. I shall try to get talking to this woman next time the alarm goes. The public prosecutor repeated, 'Next? Well?' A voice from the dark throng at the back: 'Ach, why bother with talk?! The public prosecutor doesn't give a shit. I've been here a year and never yet noticed the public prosecutor helping any of us.' Another voice shouted: 'Nothing but play-acting, get what I mean?' The public prosecutor blushed scarlet. 'Who was that?' But no one answered. It was impossible to determine which of the hundred and fifty women had spoken. Instead, he opted to leave. A good many cursed him as he went. When he had gone Frau Sch. the warder

* The German Supreme Court. In spite of what this name may suggest, the *Reichsgericht* lacked the supreme authority of the People's Court (see note on page 6). (Translator)

came. 'Just you wait,' she shrieked at Frau S., 'I'll get even with you for that. A fine thing, levelling accusations at a warder.' 'Och,' answered Frau S., 'just *you* wait. One day . . .' 'One day what?' 'Nothing, I didn't say a thing.' We grinned. Frau Sch. retreated, ranting; from beyond the bars, already in safety, she shouted, 'I'll see to it that you stay in your cells next time the alarm sounds. Riff-raff like you don't need any air-raid precautions. You'd be no great loss. Better if the bombs'd clear away some of you rabble.' I leapt angrily to my feet, but Frau P. held me back. 'It's pointless,' she said. 'In the Bible it is written that the Lord will come down and . . .' Unfortunately I cannot remember these Biblical sayings.—I've come to the end of my paper. I shall have to see about getting some more. First I shall write on the wrapping paper in the cupboard. The toilet paper (old registers of criminals) can also be used on the reverse and at the edges.

3 November 1944

Since yesterday I have no longer been in my solitary cell but in with four others. I left my peaceful cell with regret. Being together with others like this has one advantage: at difficult times you don't feel so lonely. Everything else is a disadvantage. The others gossip, you get no peace, at night they use the bucket four or five times, very noisily, one of them has diarrhoea, another stinks of some rub-on tincture or other, one wants to have the window open at night, another has rheumatism and wants it shut, and so on. This large room is even colder than my cell was. There is still no heating. Outside there is already snow on the ground. This year it has turned cold unusually early. At night I can scarcely sleep for the cold. My cough and my kidney pains are unbearable.

They are curious creatures, these women I am in with. Maria was brought in only yesterday, a plump little cook, from the munitions factory at H. She gave us a confused account of her innocence, or guilt. Apparently she stole food from the camp kitchen. It's the same thing everywhere. Resi, a buxom girl with the figure and profile of a Greek woman – whenever she opens her mouth to speak you are staggered by her stupidity. Her eyes are sad and hunted. She already has two illegitimate children by different men, and isn't sure whether or not she's expecting a third now. She is mixed up in a bad affair. She got to know a young man, a soldier, who said he was on leave. They quickly fell in love, he lived with her and brought her large quantities of food every day, and they got engaged. It was a splendid life, for about six weeks. Until one day the police turned up and took away the bridegroom and the bride as well. The young man was a deserter and, as if that wasn't enough, had been feeding himself and Resi with stolen food. Resi claims she knew nothing about all that. She is so stupid I wouldn't put it past her. She lies fully dressed on her bunk and sobs continuously. When her handkerchief is wet through she washes it out in the wash-bowl and lies on it to get it dry. She's by no means grieving for her beloved, though – she has not yet realised the fate that awaits him. She is vexed at him for having landed her in this fix, she calls him a beast, a dog, and a deceiver, and has forgotten her love. What torments her most is the thought that she might possibly be pregnant again.

The fourth is Frau H., fifty-five, Austrian, amply built, her hair dyed a strawberry blonde. She told me her story right away yesterday, the very first evening. When she was still very young she started as a chambermaid in a hotel in Holland, then was a waitress in Zurich, and God knows where else she was. She had two illegitimate children. Her father fell in the First World War. She had to feed her children all on her own, and managed it. She became a masseuse and then a swimming-pool attendant. She knows all the big spa resorts and a number of prominent people. She knows amusing stories and is surrounded by a whiff of worldliness, or, to put it more precisely, of perfume, curiosity, lechery, decadence, the intimacy of the boudoir, scandalous tales, and corruption – even if she herself never got round to experiencing anything but hard work. But she has seen part of the world, thoroughly and all too clearly, as only the eyes of chambermaids and pool-women see it – it is not a nice world, but the anecdotes she tells us are entertaining. I am interested to hear that she massaged Marie von Ebner-Eschenbach in Vienna. Her tales from a world of wealth, the good life and indolence seduced us yesterday evening into indulging our fantasy: we drew up menus, for instance oxtail soup, saddle of venison with creamed potatoes and redcurrant jelly, omelette soufflée and the appropriate wines. Frau H. knows about these things. The watered semolina soup last night had caught and was barely edible. We were terribly hungry.—Frau H. is a 'political' prisoner. Though in fact her crime seems pretty ridiculous and her political attitudes distinctly dubious. She is one of the old Salzburg 'illegals', that is to say, one of the pioneers of National Socialism in Austria. On that account she was arrested once before, in 1938, and spent four months in the castle of Hohensalzburg. Her son, I gather, is not only a teacher but also a party official. At the moment he is in Norway, and she has no news of him. Now she has been accused of listening to prohibited radio broadcasts. She tells us a long, tangled story about a malicious landlord and landlady who wanted her out of her flat at all costs, spied on all her comings and goings, and now maintain that Frau H. repeatedly listened to the Swiss station. Frau H. complains of rheumatism and severe heart pains. After she was arrested she was again examined by the relevant official doctor to see whether her health would be up to serving a sentence. He wrote her a certificate stating she was only 'fit for short-term detention'. Given my experiences here, I doubt if they will take any notice of that.

The most interesting woman here is without doubt Lotte Sch. She is thirty-three. Her figure is excellently proportioned, sporty, but terribly thin. Her face is narrow, pure, bright. The natural brown of her skin manages to dispel the impact of her sickly pallor. Till now she was in a solitary cell for two months, stitching straw footwear, which incidentally is a pretty laborious job and needs strong hands. Yesterday evening she said not a word to us at first. She stalked up and down the cell, taking long strides, until Frau H. implored her to give up her racing about. At this she leapt onto the table in one bound (here we even have a proper table) and sang the aria of Amneris from *Aïda*. She has a wonderful alto voice. We listened enthralled, until we were afraid a warder would hear her. We are strictly forbidden to sing. Everything that could be even the smallest comfort to us is forbidden. Then we sat down on Lotte's bunk and she sang one popular song after another, from 'Sous les toîts de Paris' and 'Ich bin vom Kopf bis Fuß auf Liebe eingestellt' to 'Lili Marleen' and 'Es geht alles vorüber'. Suddenly she jumped to her feet

42

and started tap-dancing. She is good at it. And all of a
sudden Resi, who till then had lain crying on her bunk, got
up too and they danced waltzes, tangos, and some dances
or other that they dreamt up, and Lotte proved to be a fine
whistler. A strangely wild mood had possessed us all. I
danced with Frau H., who can dance a Vienna waltz as
marvellously as only Austrians of the pre-War generation
can, till she was almost faint from it. Meanwhile one of us
was constantly keeping watch at the cell door. But we
remained undisturbed. When it grew dark Lotte suddenly
approached my bunk. 'May I?' she asked, and lay down
next to me. 'I'm so frozen,' she said. I shifted over a little
and waited. At length, when nothing followed, I started a
conversation. Whereupon I learnt a muddled tale, parts
of which don't fit very clearly together, but the heart of
which is doubtless true. It is bitter enough.

Lotte is the daughter of some minor Munich official.
Lotte wanted to study but they hadn't the money. So she
began to read, and she read Faust and Zarathustra,
Mendel's theory of genetics, and every conceivable work
in the natural sciences. As she was hungry for knowledge,
and clever, she retained a good deal of it all, but as she was
unfamiliar with any method of intellectual work most of it
remained half-digested and full of loose ends. At last she
took singing lessons. She seems to have found some
patrons or other who got her to the National Theatre in
Munich as a choir girl. But one day she hit on the idea of
going solo. Quickly she learnt to dance and tried to start
up a kind of vaudeville with some other unknowns.
Of course it folded instantly. Then she put in her name
for a course in gliding, and was accepted too. The course
finished and she expected an appointment as a gliding
instructress. Up to this point everything is more or less in

order. Now comes the big break. At this time, within the last few years, she seems to have experienced something decisive, some shock. She speaks of this only obliquely, in a mixed-up and mysterious way. The fact was that she no longer had anything to live on. She now changed jobs in rapid succession: apprentice to a sempstress, mannequin, an extra with Bavarian Films, secretary, and God knows what beside – last of all she called herself a sempstress. She went from village to village taking in sewing work. But she couldn't sew. She cut up the materials and made herself scarce. At last, she says, she lay out in the sun at the Chiemsee for a few days, waiting for something to happen. And something did happen: she was arrested as a con-woman. But the break in her life lay further back. There seems little doubt that at some earlier time, probably six years ago, she had an attack of some mental disorder. She was put into a psychiatric clinic and, as she was very poor, was used as a guinea-pig. Her statements relating to this period in her life are marred with outbursts of hatred. She says some professor was trying to demonstrate that injections of tubercle bacilli into the uterus can call forth a certain kind of mental illness. She was used for the tests. What was more, for some obscure reason she had count-less spinal taps, till in the end she really was mad. Finally they planned to gas her, but at this point she escaped.

If only half of all this is true, the heart of the matter seems to me to lie here – I know the horrors that go on in lunatic asylums.—I am immensely sorry for Lotte. She is hysterical, unpredictable, argumentative, yet everything she might have been (if only someone had taken her part early on) comes across vividly. It must have been toward midnight when she finally crawled onto her own bunk.

44

My lawyer was here again yesterday. He came late, and had no news for me. My files, he says, are with the Gestapo in Munich, and it may take a few more weeks before they are sent back. I had a fit of rage and said he ought to be speeding up the business but instead was letting everything take its course in its own slow way. He shouted at me to get another lawyer. I said, 'Fine, I shall.' But before I was out the door he called me back and began to complain that he felt like a man who, in his sleep, wants to call out and run but can't. This feeling of paralysis, of powerlessness in the Third Reich was unbearable, he said, and the lot of political prisoners, above all, touched his heart, but as a rule it was precisely for them that you could not do a thing. In closing he promised to arrange a talk with Gestapo Lieutenant-Colonel R. It may possibly be of some use. You clutch greedily at anything that might mean salvation, or a speeding up of things, or even only a change. It was not until shortly before half-past six that I was called in to him, along with five others. We had to wait in the icy-cold ground-floor hall, which is always draughty, till the lawyer had dealt with the men. They stood waiting beyond the bars. A warder went up and down, watching us to see we did not exchange words or even glances with the men. Among the prisoners is a tall, self-confident-looking man. Frau S., the woman from Bremen, whispered to me that he is an SS major who has committed some political crime. She didn't know what. He was in with the lawyer for an endlessly long time. The clock struck seven and then quarter past, and still he wasn't done. We were shivering with cold. The warder went into the office to warm up. Thick logs of wood were cracking and crackling in there. The kitchen women went by, steaming pots of tea in their hands. My cold was tormenting me. Frau S. and I cowered in a recess by the bars, to warm each other up. One of the male prisoners waiting there softly began a conversation. He is the ringleader of a gang of five lads from R. who have also been arrested on political charges. They seem to be on the 'left', at all events the tall one makes no secret of his hatred of the Nazis. Along with the others he has composed a 'grace before meals' in which he thanks Hitler for depriving us of all we had, one thing after the other, fat, eggs, sugar, flour, and finally even the bowls to eat from, but – and this is the refrain (unfortunately I cannot remember the exact wording) – we thanked the Führer for all the love he shows us. It is quite bitter and rebellious. He wrote this grace on scraps of paper and slipped it into letter-boxes, and at last they got on his trail. I have the impression there is more to it than this, something he doesn't want to talk about, but he whispered to me that their case was in the hands of the *Volksgerichtshof* and was being treated as high treason, and it wasn't unlikely that – he mimed being hanged. The next moment he was again telling a political joke which unfortunately I couldn't hear the end of as the warder returned. He shooed us into our corner, chased us ten metres from the men and shouted: 'Hussies – that'd be the very thing for you, wouldn't it, flirting with the men. Don't look at them! Even in prison they try to get up to things. Even Dachau's too good for you pack.' I gave him a malevolent glare, and he promptly caught my gaze and started to bombard me with abuse and swearing. In the end we all had to turn with our faces to the wall and stay standing like that. Gradually we froze to ice. The warder couldn't bear the cold for long and withdrew to his warm room. At last the SS major was ready. The tall fellow was dealt with considerably faster, and for us there remained a few minutes. The lawyer growled at Frau H., the last, when she entered, 'What do you want *this* time? I can do nothing for you.' It was almost nine o'clock when we were finally through. The lawyer left. The warder took the men to their cells and went. The lights were put out, all but a small lamp. 'Fräulein Sch. will be coming soon to let you go up,' said the senior officer, and went too. We waited, frozen stiff, tired, coughing. At last Fräulein B., the assistant wardress, came. 'Coming,' she said, 'be with you right away,' as she whisked by. She disappeared into the office. We heard loud laughter and the crackling of the fire. It was past nine o'clock by the time we were finally fetched.

During that hour, I experienced in my whole being what my understanding had grasped years before: the coldness, indifference, and brutality of the world. Today I'm lying in bed. I have stabbing pains in my chest, and on top of that diarrhoea, a cough and cold. The cell is cold. At lunchtime I was given only tea. It is some herbal tea or other, not even camomile tea. It may be that eating nothing is good for diarrhoea; but hunger is even worse than diarrhoea. The only thing that is pleasant is being alone at last for once.

Resi just came, the deserter's bride. She felt ill while she was at work. Now she is lying crying silently on her bunk, now and then totters to the bucket and throws up, and groans for fear of perhaps being pregnant. I am sorry for her. She will be given a long sentence, and after all only acted out of stupidity and love. She is uninhibited, sensual, and capable of giving herself totally. When she was already deeply entangled in love she discovered her lover

47

was a deserter. What is she being punished for now? For her stupidity and her blind love, for thinking honour is simply honour, nothing more, and love is everything.

How readily I passed judgement on people before. Now I see every human being caught as if in a net. In one's case the net may be poverty, in another's emotion and passion, in another's thoughtlessness and blundering. Many transgressions have been committed in a condition that is more a matter for a psychiatrist than for a judge. Many crimes would without doubt never have been committed at all if the structure of society were more humane to the individual, if our over-valuation of property and security were done away with.

All these crimes are today punished with prison sentences ranging from police custody of four, eight or twelve weeks to prison, detention centre, and concentration camp. While he serves his sentence, everything is done to bring home to the prisoner his criminality, his inferiority, his exclusion (through his own fault) from free human society, in an emphatic, naked, and thorough manner. A short-term sentence may not have serious consequences for the prisoner's sense of himself and moral behaviour. A longer sentence, however, is certain to be demoralising. Here in prison you turn out the very opposite of what you ought to become. You become anti-social. If once you are excluded from society, you begin to exclude yourself from it. You unlearn responsibility, for here you have none. Nor do you want it any more. You become familiar with a wicked, furtive hatred of your oppressors, you become a hypocrite, you learn to steal if you hadn't learnt it already. You learn malicious revenge, you carry out a hundred petty acts of revenge, and gradually you lose your awareness of human dignity and turn into a beaten, malevolent, servile, dulled animal. You need vast spiritual reserves to remain a human being here. Only in prison do you get to know your evil instincts. I have been watching this in myself: what I mostly desire is food, small comforts got underhandedly such as my second blanket, which I pinched from an open cell as I'm so cold; I hate the wardresses, at times I feel the overpowering urge to shove one of them down the stairs when she's in front of me. I am growing rebellious, dark, spiteful, and inconsiderate. Thus (for example) today I swapped my hard mattress for Resi's softer one. No one saw me do it.

Would it not be a thousand times better to get rid of prisons and detention centres? There are some kinds of criminals you have to put away: incorrigible anti-social elements. The remainder, whose crimes consist in having done harm to others, whether individuals or society as a whole, should make good the damage, either by paying or by working for society.

Would it not be a thousand times better to have labour camps in place of prisons, where the prisoners would have relative freedom, would be treated humanely and never unjustly or humiliatingly, and would acquire a sense of performing important and atoning work for society? People are never improved by humiliation, by crushing them, but by education, by raising their awareness of themselves and by correctly guiding their energies. If that could only be understood for once.

6 November 1944

I am still in bed. A change in our cell: the small, round cook has been sent to work outside, at the factory M., and in her place Marie H. has joined us, and requires us to call her Mariechen. She is a servant girl, an Austrian servant of the good old variety, but as far as her erotic life is concerned she is very easy. She is married, her husband is in the SS, somewhere out in the war. She has been having an affair with a Frenchman. Her discomposure gave away that it was not only that that led to her being arrested, but she was not particularly forthcoming. She laughed and cried alternately, seems on the hysterical side, and is plainly hot for men. In the course of the afternoon I discovered quite a few things more amid the laughter and tears, in scraps, obliquely and full of contradictions. What seems to be a fact is this: that the Frenchman got her pregnant, and she tried to get hold of a preparation from a doctor to bring on an abortion – early enough, at a time when the doctor could not yet definitely ascertain whether she was pregnant and it might have seemed innocent enough for her to complain of symptoms and irregularities in her period. She got the preparation, but it didn't work. Instead she found a helpful friend who straightaway succeeded in terminating the pregnancy. After a short while the doctor seemingly heard a rumour to this effect. He reported Mariechen, probably to cover himself, for he had after all given her the preparation and she, talkative and foolish, had blabbed about it. So she was charged with a twofold crime. Abortion is severely punished in the Third Reich. Mariechen told me about her life. Her husband, the SS sergeant, frequently beat her and once tried to poison her. One day on holiday he informed her that he had a lover, she was expecting his child, but he would not agree to a divorce. She tried to make a scene, whereupon he struck her and left. She followed him. In a dismal town in Saxony she found him and his lover. God knows how Mariechen managed to move him to spend a few nights with her in a hotel. Her husband (she said) was charming and one evening brought her a beer in bed, then she fell asleep. When she awoke she was alone and in terrible pain. The doctor established that she had been poisoned. When her husband returned – he had presumably been fixing himself an alibi for his whereabouts that night – she couldn't bring herself to prefer charges against him, but she blackmailed him with the threat of doing so. Now there was peace for a while. And then there was 'this damned business'. Her husband made her tremble. This is what she told me about her arrest: the village policeman took her away when she was just busy with the laundry. He took her in her work-clothes and clogs; he did not allow her to take the most necessary things with her, she was not even permitted to say goodbye to her little daughter, who was alone in the flat. When she tried to soften him up with begging and tears he struck her and called her a 'Frenchie-girl, a whore and an old sow'. Her story reminded me vividly of my own arrest, which admittedly was less uncouth but in fact had all the more dangerous aspects to it. I did not add this passage until summer 1945. On 12 October K. had gone to Salzburg. At half-past seven in the morning a gendarme appeared and, with some embarrassment, requested me to accompany him to the village for a little questioning. He preferred not to say any more. I was somewhat vexed, but still unsuspecting. When I took my leave of the children my heart suddenly grew heavy as a stone and I had a premonition of what would happen. At the inn I was questioned by two policemen. The charges covered four pages. It was a political denunciation. The charge began with my giving cigarettes to Russian prisoners of war, said I considered Hitler a megalomaniac and called him a war criminal, said I had repeated the circumstances under which Hitler came to power, that I ardently hoped Germany would somehow or other come to her senses one day and throw out the Nazis along with their capitalism and nationalism, etc. – often very naive things that I couldn't help smiling at, since they gave only a distorted image of the dangerous truth I knew – ending in the serious charge of defeatism and high treason. I had agitated against the war. This interrogation, which began at eight in the morning, lasted till two in the afternoon. I had still not eaten. My head was completely clear. I was quite at one with myself. From the start, with the first charge, I felt something that resembled the sudden starting of a mechanism, say that of a clock. I didn't let them confuse me, made light of the one point and conceded the next, though not without making it appear harmless, and bluntly denied the most serious charges, without contradicting myself. Several times I reviewed the situation in a flash, my own and the overall political situation, and each time I was on the verge of crying out, 'Of course, you idiots, I said every word of it, and more beside. Take me prisoner! I despise you and every syllable I breathe in my own defence.' But each time I reflected, 'And if they execute me? The war will be over in a few months. It's pointless being a martyr now. No, I shall save myself. I have better things to do than die. I want to live and work.' And cold-bloodedly I went on denying the charges. The interrogation lasted until two o'clock, then one of the policemen left to telephone the *Landrat*.* I wanted to use the break to collect my mail but was told not to move from where I was. Five minutes later the gendarme came back.

* The head of a regional administration. (Translator)

He said, 'You're under arrest.' At that moment I was close to fainting, but I got a grip on myself right away and asked him if I could go home just once more. Escorted by both policemen, I was taken home. I had a little time to myself. This was very decent of the two policemen. Hastily I cleared away the most suspect letters, pamphlets, books and manuscripts, shoved a good number of letters into the stove – unfortunately quite valuable ones, but far too incriminating – and pushed the rest under the sofa springs. I was expecting a Gestapo house-search. Then I ate, comforted L., who had been looking after my children in the mean time and was bawling, played with the unsuspecting children, and chatted to one of the officers while the other got on with business of his own. The afternoon passed painfully slowly. At last it was time to leave for the train. I took the children to my aunt, gave the necessary instructions, and, still under escort, went to the station. The train arrived. K. got down, I instantly pulled him into the train and rapidly whispered to him the necessary measures, told him about my interrogation, and impressed my replies upon him. In just five minutes he was fully informed. In F., the next station, we alighted. At nine o'clock we reached the police station. K. was questioned too, as he also faced charges, but his were less serious than mine and he remained at liberty. This was a considerable weight off my mind. At ten o'clock a gendarme took me to the detention room: a cellar-like room with a straw bunk with dirty blankets, no light, ice-cold. The panes in the heavily barred windows had been smashed and the cold air breezed in. The floor and walls were inconceivably filthy. Everywhere there were cigarette ends, scraps of paper, splashes of excrement, and all manner of muck. The sympathetic gendarme gave me a candle-stump. K. held me close. 'Chin up,' he said, and, when he had given me one more look, the door was closed, and the chain and keys clattered. I was a captive. I wrapped myself in a blanket, smoked a cigarette and thought over the situation. Then, exhausted, I fell asleep. When I awoke it was morning. I had slept deep and sound the whole night through. The policeman brought me water to wash and surreptitiously gave me a piece of bread, then he accompanied me to the train. K. got on at K. Once again the gendarme was very decent. He left K. and me alone and went to sit in the next compartment. We talked over every point once more, committed my exculpating answers to memory, and thought over everything K. proposed to do. At ten o'clock we were in Traunstein, where the first thing we did was to breakfast together with the gendarme. Then I said it was time and I wanted to get to the prison. Sooner or later I had to do so. K. and the gendarme took me there. K. left. I waved to him again from the window of the admissions office. Then the iron door between us clunked shut. First I was left waiting for an hour and no one took any notice of me. Suddenly a pale, short, fat man with an intelligent face asked me my name. When I gave him my maiden name he exclaimed: 'What a coincidence, I know your father!' Immediately I supposed I could sniff a chance here, but the man is himself only an inmate. He is a former bank manager and local historian from Passau. He wanted to publish a book himself, and took money for the project from the bank, in the certain belief that he would be able to pay it back immediately the book appeared. But the Law was faster than he was: he was arrested for embezzlement. Three and a half years in gaol. Now he is working in the office here. He is pale, true, but well nourished. In the meantime I have found out that

54

he is a favourite with the kitchen women and they feed him. He lives in relative comfort. At length a senior officer showed up and began by taking away my money, down to the last pfennig, then she had my name, age and marital status recorded, and finally she nodded to me to follow her. In silence we climbed four flights of stairs. Every flight ended at a heavy barred grille, and every time a grille clanged shut behind me I started. I was not yet used to it. From behind the bars of the men's section a face stared at me. The pallid, emaciated, sad face of a little Chinese. I smiled at him, touched. The wardress screeched at him: 'Get away there, Chinkie, you yellow beast, move on.' And to me she said: 'We'll have none of this smiling, mark you that. No flirting in here. Those days are over.' I thought this a crude attempt at a stupid joke and smiled. But that was my second infringement of prison rules. 'What are you laughing at? You'll be laughing the other side of your face in a while!' she yelled at me. I shrugged my shoulders and was pleased when at last we were in what was termed the effects room. I had to open the case in which I'd brought underwear, a couple of dresses and books with me. 'This all stays here!' the wardress growled as she rummaged through the suitcase. At last she tossed me one set of underclothes, a pair of stockings, and a night-dress. 'There,' she said, 'that'll be plenty for you till you get your prison clothes. And now get yourself undressed.' I gaped. 'Undressed? What for?' She shouted: 'Don't ask such stupid questions. Strip your things off.' I began hesitantly to take off my clothes. Clearly she was trying to crack a joke when she said, 'We have all the prisoners strip because we have to check if they have scarlet fever.' I stared at her uncomprehendingly and she roared out a coarse laugh. When at last I was

55

naked she took a look at me from all sides, grabbed hold of my hair, removed the hair-grips, and had me open my mouth. Finally she was done. I was spared closer examination. Others even had their genitals prodded to check for objects that might be concealed there. This I did not learn till later. One prisoner smuggled in poison in this way, another even managed money and a small watch. At last I was dressed again. The wardress removed my rings and watch, but – something she didn't incline to do with everyone – she allowed me to keep my wedding ring on. Then she enquired, 'So you're a writer, what d'you write, huh?' I told her reluctantly, albeit with the faint hope that that way I might gain her interest and a little consideration. But that was a delusion. A minute later she shoved me into the cell so roughly that I practically fell flat. Then I was on my own. Since then three weeks have gone by.

7 November 1944

Today I visited the doctor. My kidney pains and the stabbing in my chest and back were becoming unbearable. Frau H. went to be examined too. During the night she had a turn with her weak heart. There were nine of us in all, four women and five men. Naturally we again had to wait outside the surgery, ten metres apart from each other. That is one of their thousand little bloody-minded ways. Three of the men had bandaged hands or arms, one was coughing, hollow and hoarse, to judge by his appearance he must be consumptive. They were in the surgery for an extraordinarily short time. We women were all new here – the rest have given up having themselves treated here. Frau H. was before me. After half a minute she came back, shook her head and sighed. Then it was my turn. The surgery is well equipped, plainly when the prison was built there were notions of treating prisoners humanely. Now it is no more than a façade. The doctor, very old, short, wizened, limping and short-sighted, nodded to me to speak while, without looking at me, he busied himself at his desk. Briefly I told him my complaints. Before I was through he said to the wardress who was present, 'Cough mixture. Next.' Before I knew what was happening I was outside again. Frau H. quickly told me in a whisper that he had said to her, 'Prison psychosis.' She told him she had a certificate from her official doctor attesting that she was fit only for short-term imprisonment. He said: 'Nothing to do with me. For the time being you'll stick it. That's that.' In the end he ordered the wardress to give her a harmless sedative. Frau H. said: 'But I don't need a sedative. My pulse is hardly beating at all.' But the wardress had bundled her out the door. Now I'm in bed again, unable to stay up. The room is icy-cold. I'm starving. Still no medicine. Still no letter, no parcel of warm vests and food. Have they forgotten me? Sometimes all that comforts me is the thought that one day, in the event that I come through this affair, I shall shape all that is happening now into a novel or story. Before, I should never have imagined that this prospect would really help me bear up in my worst hours. But the secret of this consolation lies in the fact that it not only reinforces my waning self-confidence but also at this very moment, while I am still caught up in what is happening, removes me to a point beyond the experience, so that I am no longer merely suffering but am already moulding the experience from some position beyond the suffering. There is no stronger power than the spirit. It seems to me to be even stronger than hunger. At least it still is now. Perhaps one day I shall feel differently about it. We just had an alarm for a whole hour. I had to get up and go to the 'air-raid shelter', which as always means the hall on the ground floor. Fräulein B. was on duty. No doubt she realised that it was unbearably cold in the hall, for she unlocked a number of empty men's cells, which are cold as well, true, but as we were herded in like sheep they soon warmed up. On the other hand, after a short time the air was so bad we could scarcely breathe. When there's an alarm the prisoners working outside come in too. Among them there are also the dyers from factory M. They are covered from head to toe with colour, some of them yellow, others red, green, brown; their faces and hair are coloured too. Some have inflamed eyes, others chapped hands and arms covered with scabs and sores. Their work is extremely hazardous to health, as the dyes are toxic. Granted, the women who do this work get half a litre of milk a day to counteract the poison, but they are nonetheless affected. Z. has already been working there for seven months. At times they are so choked up with dye-dust that for all their hunger they cannot get anything down. It is by no means dangerous prisoners that are sent to work there, nor even particularly strong ones either. They are picked out at random as the need arises. I met the 'Raphael Madonna' again. She is wearing trousers, a torn shirt half-open at the breast as there isn't a button left on it, and flung round her shoulders a ragged, dusty jacket. She and her husband are separated. About half of the women here, those who are not still girls, are either divorced or in the process of getting divorced. The long separation of man and wife caused by evacuation and military service, the temptation to flirt with prisoners of war who are far stronger, healthier and more charming than the hunted, overworked German men who have been drained of their energies by the war, and further the greed for a hasty enjoyment of life which we encounter in catastrophes– all this is too much for these pretty, lonely, unguarded women. In the case of the women who have already been here longer, things are often different. The men got a divorce when their wives were arrested. They were ashamed of having wives in prison, or they were afraid their careers would be rendered impossible by a wife who was in gaol. Frequently, no doubt, the men used this opportunity as a pretext to get rid of wives they had long tired of. In this case women are the guilty parties in the divorce, get no money, usually lose the children and are wholly without means of defence. After all, the judges are men.

The cell we were locked up in is the cell where those taken with fits can cool off. The door is barred, the chains, bolts and locks are double, the windows small and double-barred, the cell is totally empty. The walls show traces of fingernails, blows and excrement. We were barely in the cell when Resi cried out loud and covered her face. On the wall behind her I saw a scratched inscription: 'Resi, I loved you. My love will go with me to my death. But you betrayed me.' Underneath, the name and date – yesterday's date. What the lad must have done and suffered to be locked up in the cell for crazies! He was not there any more. Perhaps he was already dead. Resi wept, beside herself.

Aircraft approached. The thunder of distant flak could be heard. Some of the explosions sent tremors through the ground. I sat in a corner squeezed against a sixteen-year-old who promised to tell me her story, the fifteen-year-old Estonian Kitty, and Mariechen and a new woman, who were having a fearful quarrel in undertones till at length they both burst into tears. From the conversation I gathered that the new one was the friend who had aborted Mariechen's baby by the Frenchman. Mariechen was accusing her of betrayal. The newcomer denied it and convincingly backed up her denial by pointing out that she didn't want to land herself in prison. She herself was now inside because seven cases of abortion had been proved against her. When the two of them had argued and cried enough they began to chatter eagerly about love, about Frenchmen, about the techniques of love, and in the end about those of abortion. The two young girls sat attentively beside them, all ears – they didn't miss a word. A sense of responsibility stirred in me and I felt like urging caution on the two experienced women, but I told myself that the girls would find it all out anyway sooner or later. Why should I obscure their view of the reality of life through a prudishness that was out of place here. Maybe it wasn't so very new to the two children in any case, because a few times they smiled in amusement. As for myself, I found out one or two new things like this, to be exact, eight methods of abortion. In here I have to put aside the remnants of my bourgeois prejudices time and again. I have never seen life as I'm getting to see it here: naked, ugly, tough, but unfaked and real. If ever I return to normal life I shall be transformed.

8 November 1944

Today I've got up again as I cannot lie on the hard bunk any longer. I still haven't been given my cough mixture. What is more, the chief officer said to me: 'Get up, you snivelling hussy, and you'll soon be feeling better. We know your sort.' So I got up, spent a miserable day in the sewing cell and was happy when Frau P. gave me a piece of bread. In the evening I got the first letter from K. It is dated 14 October. Today is 8 November. Frau P. told me the letters are first sent to the Gestapo in Munich, then back to the magistrate's court here, and from there to the prison. The court censor's stamp is dated 1 November. Frau P. said the letters are just left lying. Often they are simply forgotten. Frequently some wardress or other neglects to pass them on to the prisoners. Thus Frau M. saw a letter addressed to herself lying in the office. She asked if she could read it right away. The duty officer refused. That evening she still hadn't been given it. The wardress forgot three days on end to give it her. This isn't a matter of malice, it is simple thoughtlessness – though in the last analysis thoughtlessness is nothing other than malice. K.'s letter is short and restrained. He writes he has sent off a food parcel. All my hopes are geared to this parcel. Today Frau M. advised me to report for outside work. One section of the prisoners is working in a bakery. It is warm there and now and then you can steal bread. I had my name given to the governor. He said that as I had not yet had my hearing he couldn't take a decision. He would first have to check with the public prosecutor. The governor, a constantly harassed man with an uncertain gaze, is not really bad, far more he's soft and not up to the job in hand. I tried to win him round. You pick that up here without really trying. Instinctively you make use of any little chance and exploit it to the best of your ability. He began to be interested in me and my story, and in the end I succeeded in obtaining permission to fetch one of the books out of my case, which I had already asked the head wardress for twice, in vain. When I saw her, I told her spitefully. 'Is that so,' she growled. 'I'll see about giving it you when I've the time.' Naturally I still haven't had it. But the prospect of having a book is wonderful. I am curious to see if I am still at all capable of reading, and whether the things that interest me at other times still have any value for me. At times, when the craving for food happens for a while not to be consuming me, I sense with amazement, shock and satisfaction that many things in my former life are no longer of any consequence to me. Now and then I take to considering my life from a perspective of death. Then I am patient, wise, heroic. Suddenly, though, a quite unheroic anguish overcomes me, a blind rage against this tyrannical regime, a wild anger at these walls, bars, and oaken doors, these hundreds of chains, bolts, locks, and security measures, this whole merciless system of dehumanization. I am dead tired, I cannot think any more, nor write, hunger is devouring me.

9 November 1944

Yesterday evening we were all in despair. There are days when – as if in response to an order, without apparent cause – we all at once take a fit of prison madness. It started with Frau H. declaring that it was true that all of this, the reign of terror and the Nazi tyranny, was dreadful, but the Führer himself was good. He didn't know what was going on, and, just as you shouldn't hold the Pope responsible for the errors of individual priests, so you couldn't blame Hitler for the errors of his party officers. You had only to think how much the Führer loved children. Someone like that couldn't be evil. I gritted my teeth and tried not to listen. But Lotte, who had had a bad day anyway, started to answer back loudly and tartly. Her arguments were not always watertight, but they were put with so real a bitterness that at first Frau H. fell silent in astonishment. Then, however, a contemptible row broke out, with Lotte and Frau H. talking at the same time and neither listening to the other. It ended with Lotte leaping onto her bed in a rage, not without first flinging the window-flap wide open, which Frau H. wouldn't have, in view of her rheumatism; and, when it emerged that we all wanted the window open, Frau H. had a turn with her heart. It soon passed, but the tension remained. Lotte sang out loud, I asked for quiet, Resi wept, Mariechen was kept forever on the bucket by her diarrhoea, the stench filled the entire cell. We snapped at her and she started crying. In the end I grew so angry about it all, not at the poor creatures here but at the fact that we are forced into such scenes, that I threw our tin bowls, my shoes and God knows what else at the wall, one thing after another. This sobered us all up, and finally we fell asleep in exhaustion. During the night we were awoken by a great din in the neighbouring cell. Fists hammered at the cell door, and a number of excited voices shouted for the duty officer. In the end the head wardress came, cursing and scolding. After a couple of minutes, things calmed down again. In the morning we discovered that Frau S., the one who knew such dangerous political jokes, had attempted suicide. She had always had a sharp razor on her, and at times she had said it was her insurance against a concentration camp. No one had taken her seriously. Tonight she had suddenly set about cutting her wrists, but in doing so she was hit by the fear of death and screamed. The wound is not a large one. But as a result they took us apart today good and proper. We had to leave the cells while a wardress ransacked every mattress, every shelf, every last corner. I trembled on account of my diary, which I have sewn into my straw bolster in such a way that I only have to open up and sew shut a few stitches in the seam at the edge of a narrow side. I watched the wardress feeling at the bolster. Of course she knows all the dodges and hiding-places. But she found nothing. Afterwards the cell was a chaotic heap of blankets, tin bowls, articles of clothing, and the other objects we are allowed. Our cell contained nothing that is prohibited. In the smithy cell, though, they found all the more: beer bottles, food, powder, nail-scissors, lipstick, hair-curlers, newspapers, cigarettes, matches, torches, and God knows what besides. When the prisoners came back from their outside work they had to strip in the hall and wait stark naked while the wardress rummaged through their clothes. They grinned, froze, bared their teeth and whispered obscenities. We saw and heard it all as our cell door was still ajar, and we squabbled fiercely and in silence over the best place at the door. From the pockets, seams and hems of their dresses a good many things came to light which I envied them for, above all cigarettes. The wardress tossed everything into a single, jumbled heap, ordered two other prisoners to take the finds to the office, and gave the convicts, who were shaking with cold, a stiff, coarse sermon consisting mainly of threats of detention and beatings, and meanwhile Z., who'd repeatedly said earlier on that she had to relieve herself but had been refused permission, suddenly and unabashed let her water stream forth, so that a vast lake appeared on the shiny parquet floor. Massive uproar.

Alarm again this morning at half-past four. Once more we were in the cell for crazies. I discovered that on each wall there were several 'letters' to Resi. Plainly the poor devil had spent the whole day scratching these love letters into the wall with his fingernails (for he had nothing else). As a large number of bombers were flying right over the town and we were all cowering rather fearfully, mute and expectant, someone began to whistle loud and cheekily. We were outraged, one and all. The whistler was a newcomer with her hair cut very short, almost like a boy. She sat astride the lid of the latrine, dangling her legs and whistling. Vexed, I said, 'Do be quiet. If I'm to be hit by a bomb I'd like to hear it coming.'

The newcomer laughed out loud in an expressionless, absent way, and went on whistling. Furiously I turned my back. Whereupon she jumped to her feet, pushed through the others and settled next to me. 'Let me tell you something,' she said, 'anyone who's been where I've been forgets about consideration. Remember that.' At that instant the planes were immediately above us. It was deathly silent in the cell. Only the window-panes rattled, owing to the blast-waves. All of a sudden the newcomer laughed harshly and cried out scornfully: 'There you all squat, shitting yourselves. Serves you right.' The rest were all too occupied with their fear of death to turn on her. Tense, I asked her softly: 'Why does it serve us right?' She leant towards me and said: 'I suppose the war isn't your own fault, huh? Wasn't it what you wanted? Didn't you vote for him, that lout, the crazy one?' I said, 'Quiet! What you're saying is dangerous.' She laughed in my face. 'I'm not afraid any more. Do you know where I've been, for five years?' Somewhere a bomb fell. The newcomer began to whistle again. Someone said crossly: 'Look, if you don't shut your mouth now I'll shut it for you.' The newcomer said contemptuously: 'No you won't – I wouldn't advise it. You try going to Auschwitz for five years.' No one made any reply to this. The bombers flew off westward; gradually the others began to talk. I started a conversation with this newcomer. Betty is twenty-six. She isn't coming completely clean, but I have the feeling she is a card-carrying member of the KPD.* She knows the ropes. The things she said about Auschwitz were even worse than what I know of Dachau, but her way of telling was disjointed and unclear and proceeded in leaps and exclamations. Often she forgot what she wanted to say and just stared ahead. At times I had the impression I was talking to someone who was mentally unhinged. She's just been saying that Auschwitz is a city of barrack buildings, with electrified barbed wire all round which prisoners frequently try to climb over, using bundles of straw for protection against the current – though almost all of them are shot. The next moment she gives me a smacking kiss and cries out: 'But this dress, I didn't have it in Auschwitz. It's from my aunt.' She laughs nervously. 'If I come across cigarette ends here in prison I'll give you one, right?' I am not remotely surprised that someone goes crazy after five years in a concentration camp. She is so nervy that her eyes are constantly twitching. Her mouth, hands and feet make unmotivated, purposeless, distracted movements. Her eyes are upsetting: Betty tries to put as impertinent an

* *Kommunistische Partei Deutschlands*, the German Communist party. (Translator)

66

expression as possible into them. But in reality they are hunted, uncertain, furtive, full of fear, and often of cold hatred. In Auschwitz she was freed because the Russians were approaching. She returned home, only to be arrested again right away. Now she is due to be sent from here to a camp again, most probably Dachau. She shouted out: 'I don't care, I don't give a shit. I don't want to live any more anyway. Out here it's just as bad as in the camp. But I tell you, one day Hitler'll pay for it. He'll hang!' Horrified, I placed my hand over her mouth and said to the others, 'Don't listen. She's quite mad. Five years of Auschwitz, think of it!' Many of them nodded in sympathy and solidarity, some shook their heads, and only Frau R., who is inside for black-marketeering and is forever talking about her friend, 'an intimate associate of our Führer', who will soon have her out of here, whispered, 'I'd advise you not to get yourself involved in anything risky. I mean well with you.' Betty sized her up from tip to toe, then said, 'So why are you inside, then?' Frau R. gave her an indignant look, sighed at such grossly ungrateful impoliteness, and turned her back. 'So why's she not telling?' demanded Betty. A voice from a dark corner: 'Oh, it's such a little bagatelle, not worth wasting words on.' Everyone roared with laughter. The voice went on: 'All she did was shift a couple of hundredweight of wurst that she'd got from our dear cook Frau A. But her boyfriend the SS major's going to get her out soon.' The others split their sides laughing. Frau R. leapt to her feet, white with anger: 'I won't have this. Who's got the right to—' 'Calm down,' said Betty, 'you're just a prisoner, nothing more.' At this, an elderly woman joined in the talk: 'I must say,' she called across, emphasising every word, 'this tone of speaking is outrageous. Who do these young folk think they are?

All of us are prisoners, it's true. But there's still a difference between a lady and a servant girl.' The woman from
Bremen, half in anger and half in amusement, called
across, 'Look here, I'm a private secretary, and this
woman next to me is a writer, to take just two examples,
Frau L.' 'Frau *von* L., if you please,' the Lady cried. We
killed ourselves laughing. My own sympathy was so much
on the side of the uncouth, cheeky, streetwise and honest
girls that I couldn't help but say: 'People like Frau *von* L.
will never understand that their *von* is the calling-card of
their stupidity.' 'Bravo,' shouted the girls. Betty gave me a
resounding kiss on the cheek. Frau von L. and Frau R. cast
me annihilating glares. Unabashed, I went on, 'People
who think like that are just as much to blame for the dirty
mess we're in as the rest.' Betty kissed me a third time and
began to whistle the Internationale. Nobody here knows
it, but still I gave Betty a startled nudge. 'Darling,' she
said, 'you've earned your cigarette-butt. You'll have to
join the KPD!'

11 November 1944

This morning I was summoned before the governor. I
supposed he was going to tell me my hearing was
arranged. He was alone in his office. 'Look here,' he said, a
little embarrassed as he always is when talking to me, 'I'd
like to give you some good advice: be careful. You're in
here for political reasons. Your case is . . . how shall I put
it? . . . it's doubly dangerous for you to talk politics
in prison.' I stared at him uncomprehendingly. He
squirmed: 'Well, you see, what you were saying yesterday
and your friendship with the woman from the camp . . . I

68

myself am convinced of your innocence.' I grinned at him. 'But,' he continued, 'there are wicked women in here. And by the way, as of Monday you can work outside, in the L. bakery.' I thanked him and promptly added that I had still not received the book he had allowed me to have. He said I should tell Fräulein B. and not the head wardress. I smiled understandingly. 'Yes, I know,' he said with a sigh, 'things aren't easy.' He is afraid of the head wardress, her machine-like correctness, her alertness. He himself would prefer in some cases to close both eyes. It is quite clear to me that he is accessible for corruption of any kind. It disgusts me, but I keep this feeling to myself, cover it up, talk myself out of it, for how else could I succeed in wangling some preferential treatment or other out of him? It is debasing, all of it. Tomorrow I shall be moving to another cell. I almost regret it because I have got on very well with the four of them, crazy as they were. They liked me. When I told them I'd be leaving them tomorrow they wept loudly. Now they plan to have a farewell celebration this evening.

12 November 1944

Sunday afternoon. The fourth Sunday in prison. This morning I cleared my bed and my few belongings into cell 50. Then I was kitted out for my outside work, in the sewing cell. So now, over the top of my own underwear (which I'm allowed to wear because there's too little prison underwear available), I'm wearing a pinafore made of faded grey cotton material that's been repaired a hundred times, and a skirt that was once a soldier's uniform and is far too roomy for me. Also I got a thick, indescribably ugly men's jacket, a blue headscarf, knee-socks with blue and red diagonal stripes, and wooden shoes. Frau P. quickly sewed my skirt tighter while I, working in the sewing cell for the last time, ironed a mountain of laundry. It was the public prosecutor's laundry. I was surprised that we prisoners have to do that. Frau M. suggested the public prosecutor's wife didn't have a servant. I flew into a rage: 'She has just the one child, doesn't she? And nothing else to do? And she can't even wash and iron her laundry? I have two children, a garden, five other people to look after, and my books* to write on the side, and I get it all done single-handed. But of course her ladyship the public prosecutor's wife uses the prisoners' help. Cheap help. Free.' I was shouting, and was sorely tempted to singe one or two articles of clothing with the hot iron, as a memento for the public prosecutor – till my humour and with it my equilibrium was restored by noticing that the public prosecutor's pillows were without exception torn to shreds at all four corners. We guessed a cat was to blame. Frau M. thought the child had done it. But to judge by the child's underwear the girl must be ten or eleven. I hit on a plausible explanation: in sleepless nights before important court sessions, the public prosecutor chews off the corners of his pillow out of nervous despair. We had a lot of fun with this notion. In the afternoon I took leave of Frau M. and Frau P., who had helped me get through many hard hours, more by their serenity than their Biblical quotations. When I returned to the cell I found myself together with six others.

* During those years I wrote the novel *Hochebene*, the novella *Elisabeth* and the children's book *Martins Reise*, none of which could of course be published at the time because I was banned from publication. They did not appear in print until after the war. (LR)

Compared with this crowd I was in quite good company with my four crazies in cell 65. They are very loud, and I find it difficult to write behind my book in my corner. At the moment they are playing blind man's buff, to keep warm. It is so dark that I can hardly see the letters I am writing. The bunk next to mine belongs to a young thing, Susi, seventeen or eighteen years old, a German from the Banat. She was a Red Cross assistant and told me a long, adventurous story to the effect that she is in prison for desertion, as she fled her Warsaw field hospital to save herself from the Russians. This isn't true. I have already heard her story from Frau M. In the field hospital she stole the parcels intended for the wounded, and furthermore she frequently spent the night with soldiers in hotels and then made off without paying, so she is quite simply a thief. What is more she is hot for men. The next two are Anni and Rosi, two of the three young girls who ran away from the munitions factory to get away to Switzerland. Likewise thieves, unpleasant creatures. The fourth is Helena, a blonde Polish woman, who is in for refusing to work. Plainly she comes of good family, at all events she seems to be quite spoilt. She pretends to be stupid, supposedly understands not a word of German, but in reality follows every word we utter alertly and acutely, and chimes in with her story again and again: 'I saying to Mister, I not able working in such bad air. I sick. Oh my lung. Oh my cough. Mister say you have to. I say, oh no, nothing having to. Mister goes to police.' This is the third time I have heard the story this evening. When we asked her to open the window below which her bed stands, she cried out indignantly: 'I doing something for you Germans? I not want.' She hates us passionately. The fifth is Käthe, also a Banat German, and the sixth

71

Anneliese, the wife of an SS captain. Now it is pitch dark.

First time working outside. At a quarter to seven in the morning we have to present ourselves in pairs in the ground-floor hall. At the front nine smithy-workers, then fifteen workers for the L. bakery, and fourteen for the M. dye-works. Every group has its own duty officer. Ours is Fräulein H., a grumpy, short, bow-legged person, not especially malicious, but stupid, nervy and unpredictable. She's called the 'prison dachshund' on account of her legs, but the nickname expresses too little of her nature. Rather, she resembles one of those excited, miffed, mistrustful, perpetually yapping rat-like little terriers that hide their own fear and insecurity with their snapping fuss. For ten minutes we stood frozen and in silence till at last the governor came with Z., the former bank manager, counted us out and called the roll. Then Huber, the prison attendant, opened the door and let us into the courtyard. There we stood for another five minutes, shivering in the cold wind. Sleet was coming down. Then at last the iron door was opened and we moved on out. Our wooden clogs clattered on the cobbles. Our route takes us through a street of imposing residences and past a café, which wakened my longing for civilisation, but when I took a closer look I saw it was no longer a café but overnight accommodation for soldiers on leave. The bakery is a small, neglected subsidiary of a larger foodstuffs factory. You pass through a narrow ante-room, where a lorry stacked with cardboard boxes takes up all the space, so

72

that we are only just able to squeeze between the wall and the wheels with difficulty. Then there is a second ante-room with movable iron trestles with hundreds of white loaves lying on them, fresh and crisp from the bakery. Our wardress took up a position from which (she thought) she could watch our every move. Nonetheless there wasn't a single one apart from me who didn't in a twinkling break off a piece of bread in passing and drop it into a pocket or sleeve. I was astounded. We could also be seen through the high glass walls of the office. A made-up blonde cast arrogant, bored glances at us, while the oven-hot bread we had filched crackled and steamed in our pockets. In my life I had seen only one foodstuffs factory, the Oetker works in Bielefeld. From that occasion I had retained an appetising image of white tiled walls, gleaming machine metal, and white aprons. Of all that I saw nothing here: a bare, grey room looking onto the coalyard and a wizened espalier pear-tree against a smoke-black wall; a few old machines, at least one of which is broken down at any given moment; disorderly heaps of flour and bran sacks in a corner, uncomfortable work-places and the stink of the coal heating – probably the smoke was welling through some holed pipe, without anything being done about it. But the room is warm, and the clatter of the two massive milling machines has something comforting and soporific about it. And what is more, it is not a prison. All of us have work to do. I was sent to a corner to mend sacks. There I sat, sewing and watching. The two blonde sisters from Northern France, the strongest of us, push in the heavy iron trestles loaded with bread, unload them and put the bread through a kind of large meat-mincer that tears it up and spits it into iron tubs, in small pieces. Every two hours these tubs are emptied into the four large drying ovens, once the bread that has already been dried has first been taken out. The roasted bread is tipped into the maw of a mill that grinds the pieces down to breadcrumbs with a loud, wooden rattling. The breadcrumbs run into sacks which are emptied into a hole in the floor from time to time. From there they are shifted by means of a paternoster into the funnel of the two filling machines, whose spouts are constantly moving up and down and spewing out a load of breadcrumbs at every move. These loads are caught in little paper bags by the two prisoners who sit there, and set aside. Two other girls take them away, hang them into a machine that seals the packets and passes them on to a table where several prisoners take them up, hastily check them over, and pile them up in stacks of five. Two packers each place ten such stacks in one cardboard box. One prisoner is occupied in folding pre-cut cardboard into boxes and stapling the finished boxes shut. Per day at least 320 boxes have to be filled, that is to say 320 times 50, in other words 16,000 packets of *L.'s Breadcrumbs*. As the work has to be done by two groups, a kind of competition is arranged to see who will hit this target figure fastest and pack the most beyond it. I am enraged at so much childish stupidity. We get nothing for this work, and naturally nothing for the over-achievement either. The bakery uses only the labour of prisoners. It runs extraordinarily cheaply. We work from seven in the morning till half-past eleven and from one o'clock till half-past five, nine hours altogether. Most factories have been shut down. This comical little factory, however, is rated as 'essential for the wartime economy' and is working at top capacity. How come breadcrumbs are essential? I am astonished. The prisoners who work in the dye factory and the smithy are given a snack twice a day: bread with

74

sausage and milk, in the smithy beer. We get nothing. We work nine hours with crisp white breadrolls. Our stomachs, which all morning long contain nothing but a few gulps of malt coffee without milk or sugar and two pieces of black bread, rumble loudly. Our hunger cannot be stilled. We are strictly forbidden to take even a single piece of bread. After ten minutes I already had a big hunk in my pocket, which someone had put my way with monkey-like speed. It tasted marvellous. I ate it so greedily that I still have stomach pains now. But if I keep warm and get a few scraps of stolen white bread every day I shall manage to keep going here for some time yet. True, the company is disagreeable: the two sloppy girls from the Banat, the two thieves Rosi and Anni, the wife of the SS captain, the two spiteful women from Northern France, a peasant girl riddled with lice, two cheeky creatures I don't yet know who lick the wardress's boots and stick out their tongues when her back is turned, a burly female at the drying oven who says she owns a big inn and claims to be a political prisoner (political is reckoned the superior thing to be), and then the buxom Versailles girl Odette, a Frenchwoman to the tips of her toes, with unbelievably nimble fingers, bright eyes, and a sharp tongue, cunning, knows all the tricks. Today, while she was having an impassioned argument with the wardress about something or other, she succeeded in stealing a piece of bread and blithely stowing it in her blouse, in front of her very eyes. Frau R. is a ray of sunshine in our crowd – she struck me that time the public prosecutor visited. She talks to nobody, haughtily and coolly ignores them all, seems to be constantly wrapped up in some important and angry reflections, and when the break comes round she walks up and down in the wet, barred-up coalyard, her hands in the

75

sleeves of her jacket. Unless I am much mistaken, she is a political prisoner. Around midday we are led back to the prison. We have to wait at the kitchen door, where we get our bowls, and then we have to wait again till the wardress lets us into our cells. Today it took so long that the food was already cold by the time we were finally sitting round the table. I had eaten so much white bread that I was full, for the first time in four weeks. Being full is a marvellous feeling, even if your stomach feels heavy. After the meal we have time off. I lay on my bed, racked by stomach pains, and wrote my diary. Now it's evening and the lights are on. Lights, for the first time. Half an hour of light. I bolted my food so that I could get on with my writing quickly. I just want to get the SS woman's story down. She has been married to an SS captain for five years and still hasn't had a child. But every SS marriage has to have produced at least one child after five years or the man can divorce his wife, indeed a divorce is obligatory whether he wants it or not. But before the divorce the woman is made to undergo all kinds of experiments. Anneliese was put in an SS hospital and examined there. After they had failed to find anything wrong, they operated on her a number of times – on occasion it was very painful (no anaesthetic) and she was always watched by a crowd of SS men (doctors and military). Then she was transferred to a sanatorium, at SS expense of course, and from there she was sent home. Her husband was given leave. All to no avail. She was subjected to renewed treatment, for months on end, time and again. She started to put up resistance, but she was in the power of the SS doctors. When the treatment had been dragging on for nearly a year she developed gynaecological disorders, which she still suffers from; you can smell it. A great many of the girls and women here have a repellent

76

smell which is not due to uncleanliness alone. And now Anneliese, having sat out four weeks in prison for illegal food-stockpiling, is to be divorced. She says, 'You've no idea what goes on in the SS. Count yourselves lucky you don't know.' Suddenly Susi, the little thief from the Banat, leapt up and shouted: 'I warn you! This is politics! It's against regulations to talk politics here. I won't have anyone say a thing against National Socialism.' I said out loud, 'Stupid cow.'

14 November 1944

K. came today. When I returned from the bakery at lunchtime I was summoned to the office. I had no idea why. K. was there. He stared at me without recognising me. He went on looking past me at the door, expecting me. I called to him, and he started. I burst into tears, fell into his arms, and wept. Now I feel ashamed that I did, but then I couldn't help it. He was given five minutes. The head wardress stood right next to us, her eyes on her watch, listening eagerly to every word. We could hardly speak. I don't know what I said or what K. said. But when he asked how I was being treated I said, to reassure him, 'Very well. The warders look fiercer than they are.' The wardress yelled at me: 'That's enough of that! It's against prison regulations to talk about officers. Just for that your time's up now – let's be having you.' K. and I looked at each other, and embraced, and then K. left. I was shattered. The wardress thrust a box at me that K. had brought, with bread, cake and apples in it, and pulled me out of the office. On the way to the cell she yapped away at me without stopping, but I barely heard a word. K. had

77

been. And he was gone again. I wish he hadn't come. I had already begun to forget freedom and sink into blissful oblivion. Now I have to come to terms with it all from scratch once again.

15 November 1944

The box K. brought me was lined with newspaper, and the papers are four to seven days old. I fell upon them greedily. The Russians seem to have got bogged down around the Plattensee, and the Allies likewise in Holland and the Vosges. Hitler's talk about victory and defending to the last drop of blood is revolting. What a tormentingly slow death Germany is dying, just so that the Nazis can cheat the gallows for half a year longer. It isn't good to think about politics in prison – the prisoner's sense of absolute impotence becomes doubly acute if you do.

An intermezzo on the way to the prison: on the narrow pavement we encountered an old man who looked like a venerable, bigoted high-school teacher. He was pretty doddering, but had on golden party insignia. We moved aside, but he poked Odette with his stick; she replied with a little harmless abuse in French. Presumably he did not understand it, but he turned, threatened us with his stick, and shouted: 'You ought to be forbidden to walk on the pavement. The pavement is for decent people, not for rabble like you.' I called out: 'I like that. We're human beings too. You don't know why we're in prison.' The warder shouted to me to shut my mouth but I added out loud: 'There's a lot of people at liberty with far better reason to be in prison than us.' Infuriated, the old man screeched: 'Impertinent into the bargain! Riff-raff! Gaol-

78

birds! They ought to beat you.' Luckily for me we turned off at that point. The old man carried on ranting for a while from behind us, while the warder called me a 'common idiot' who 'goes round offering cheek to old gentlemen'. I laughed out loud with anger and pride and said, 'You wouldn't understand such things, Fräulein H.' At this she swore again like a fishwife, but words can't hurt. The old gentleman with his golden party insignia made my entire hatred of the regime flare up anew.

At the bakery today I was ordered to the packing table as the girl with the lice had been released. I had imagined the work would be easy, but I soon realised that you have to learn everything. You need to work very fast or the packets heap up into a terrible pile. I put on quite a spurt, but after two hours I noticed blood on the packets I was stowing, and when – puzzled – I checked up I found that both my arms had been chafed raw at the wrists by the sharp edges of the boxes. My hands are swollen and, since the work has to be done standing, I have very bad kidney pains once again. My cough (I've still not been given any mixture) has got worse too, as my feet always get wet along the way. I don't yet have the knack of walking right in the heavy wooden clogs. Instead of a hundred and sixty boxes I managed only a hundred and thirty. To my astonishment I found I was angry at this, in spite of what my reason told me.

I cannot go on writing even though we have the light, I am too tired and my hands are hurting.

My lawyer came today. My files have still not arrived. He thinks K. should try to go to the Gestapo in Munich in person. I'm against this plan. He would be better keeping well clear of it all. But why am I being kept in here without any hearing? I am in despair. My lawyer is doing nothing, nothing, nothing. He wrings his hands and complains about the legal system in the Third Reich, the impotence of lawyers and defence counsel, the war, everything. But none of that is any help to me. I want to get out of here, soon, I can't stand it any more. I am nervous, tetchy, and have a cold. My lawyer shrugs his shoulders. 'Pity, but that's how it is. Difficult, but what am I to do?' I have given him various addresses to contact. My lawyer notes down everything placidly, his eyes gleam, he slams his fist on the table and exclaims, 'An excellent idea. Why didn't we have it before?' I said, 'Herr M., you know as well as I do that it's no good. You're a professional consoler.' He looked at me nonplussed, then he laughed and pulled a pear out of his briefcase and gave it me. I accepted it – why not? He could really have brought three or four. But still: he was breaking the rules in giving it to me. Also he'd brought me a few small books to choose from. I picked a yellow Ullstein novel by Vicki Baum (he knows she is banned, and I was pleased), Stendhal's *Abbess of Castro*, and a little French tale. The lawyer has taste. I suspect that in private (his passion is for history) he is quite amusing, but he's less so as a lawyer. And yet: that gesture, those books, a brief conversation which for once was not about prison and my files but about literature, made me happy for five minutes. My God, how badly (now I notice it again for the first time) I'm missing an

80

intellectual life. I put the books in my knickers, there wouldn't have been any other way of getting them to my cell.—

I was just about to start reading when my attention was taken by Käthe's story. Käthe is just sixteen years old, a monster of a lass, big, fat, ugly, gap-toothed, half a child and half a talented cheat. She has quite an adventurous story, and it has the ring of truth. Käthe's parents have a medium-sized estate and inn somewhere in the Banat. When Käthe was about eight her parents took a trip to relatives in Stuttgart. The child was so powerfully impressed by Germany, or to be exact by the big city, that for years she could think of nothing but returning there. But her parents would not let her. And in any case the war broke out, and there were no passports to be had, at least not by her. So one night she upped and away with a little suitcase, aiming for the border. For three days she looked for the border. She didn't dare ask the way. One day she saw an elderly man in an inn and casually asked him the way to a village she knew was close to the border. The man laughed. He wanted to get across the frontier too. Käthe promptly thought up a plan: she'd be his daughter and he'd be a cattle dealer. For a good deal of money they hired a cart and a horse, and blithely rode to the frontier village on the pretext of doing business there; but then Käthe had second thoughts. It was better to go over on her own. The frontier was very carefully watched, and Käthe assumed her parents had alerted the border guards. So she deserted her 'father' and waded and swam across a river by night, right next to the customs post. When she had practically reached the bank they started shooting. But since she had already set foot on Austrian soil the shooting was immediately stopped. She told the German officials she was a political refugee. They took her to a guard-room, where for a good while she was left unsure what was to happen to her, till in the end she abruptly decided to run away. She succeeded, and travelled to Vienna on the Budapest–Vienna express with a platform ticket, locking herself in the toilet. In Vienna she just stood blubbing and howling on the platform. The NSV took care of her. Suddenly all she could speak was Hungarian. They got her an interpreter, and she told the interpreter she wanted to go to Germany. She had lost her parents, who had travelled to Stuttgart. She knew the address. One day later she was sitting in the Vienna–Stuttgart train, with a ticket provided by the NSV and with food and money. And so in the end she did indeed get to Stuttgart. From there she wrote home. Her parents ultimately gave their blessing and sent her some money. Käthe went to the college of commerce and had just got a job as a shorthand typist when she hit on the idea of black-market dealing. She was fifteen and a half years old. Her friend, a sales girl at a butcher's, gave her meat coupons, and she exchanged these for an even greater number of fat coupons. These she swopped for underwear. The supply of coupons grew and the deals became ever more lucrative. She sold the underwear and started acquiring dresses, coats, and shoes with money and food. When she had filled four suitcases she decided to take a holiday back home. First she had to go to the Hungarian consulate, which is in a village near here, and that was her downfall. She had problems with her passport and presently, for reasons she wasn't told, they had her open one of her cases; in the end she discovered that a charge had been brought against her in Stuttgart and had followed her the whole way, as it were. When she was brought to prison she was in possession of eight pairs of new shoes, two suits, three coats, ten dresses and mountains of silk underwear, all of it very expensive and brand new. She told us that at her hearing the judge asked her about the contents of her cases. She confessed everything. She was shown the cases and the dresses. Among them was an evening gown with lace and pearls. The judge asked her in all seriousness if the dress had suited her. 'Sure,' she replied in her broad Swabian dialect, 'of course, I looked real swell, you bet, your honour. The boys fair broke their necks turning to look.' The judge said he could well believe it. We wept with laughter. I think that K., if her spirit of adventure, her enterprise, and her genius for a good deal are guided into the proper channels, will turn out a first-rate businesswoman.

17 November 1944

Red Cross sister Susi has been moved to the prison at L. on remand. Thank God. Her place in our cell has been taken by a burly landlady, B. She has been inside for eight months now and says she is a political prisoner. She trafficked in foods and also made dubious political comments. Be that as it may. She was in Stadelheim for seven months and has told us various stories about it. In Stadelheim they execute by decapitation. The guillotine is in the courtyard. Prisoners who have transgressed against prison rules in some way have to mop up the blood from the guillotine by way of punishment. The executions take place during the night, at four o'clock, and in the morning the guillotine has to be clean again.

Now and then the prisoners got a slice of blood sausage, which they all devoured with immense relish. If new inmates joined them, the old hands would say quite casually, pointing to the sausage, 'They executed quite a few last night.' The newcomers didn't eat a morsel of the sausage and the veterans were triumphant over their double rations. She went on to tell us she had an old head wardress who was very Catholic. Every Sunday they had mass and the prisoners sang, and anyone who was particularly keen on church attendance, prayed and sang especially loudly, and uttered pious speeches, was given preferential treatment by the old woman. Naturally everyone crammed into the church and sang forth, all the while whispering dirty jokes and, to compensate for their mock-saintliness, swearing blasphemously behind their prayer-books.

I should add that Frau B., the landlady, is our newspaper too and our press office. At the factory she has to work at the heating as well as at the drying oven. In this way she regularly has contact with the bakers, civilian workers, and from them she learns what's new. Today, for example, she told us that the Allies are marching on Lindau, that Switzerland gave them the right of passage. I believe this to be nonsense, but foolishly it offers me a glimmer of hope too.

When we had the alarm today I at last met Mariechen and the little fat cook from H. again. The cook has had her trial. She was given eleven months. She cried and swore she was innocent. There were four witnesses to her alleged thefts, and all four taken together were reckoned as one witness turned state's evidence. Her lawyer had advised her to plead guilty at the trial; he felt the war would soon be over and she would on no account need to sit out her entire sentence. He advised her not to make the trial difficult by denials. She would get a far lighter sentence if she confessed. And now she had got eleven months. She was in despair. 'But I really am innocent,' she shouted. R., the short disagreeable thief, had her trial today too. Eight months. She had my lawyer for her defence. She told us that beforehand she'd eavesdropped on a conversation among the judges. They had decided on eight months for her. The public prosecutor had demanded a year and a half. The lawyer made a magnificent speech and knocked the sentence down to eight months. They agreed, reluctantly, in view of her youth. R. poured forth the most terrible abuse of her lawyer, every judge under the sun, and the entire world. There is a lot of real and naked bitterness in this fickle creature. I met Mariechen again too. She looks in a wretched way, pale, thinned-down, and ragged. She has had a series of interrogations. A policeman told her it would be better if she confessed everything and she could go ahead and tell him all of it, he'd see the whole business went well, he realised she was a poor tormented woman and the judges would understand that too. And Mariechen, overwhelmed by his goodness, told him everything she'd hitherto been denying so obstinately. She owned up to her abortion. Of course she's in it now good and proper, because her confession was recorded as a statement without her fully grasping what was going on. She was taken to the interrogations (at the police station) by a young SS man. Mariechen is attractive to a particular kind of man, for all her raggedness. The SS man eyed her up and said that if she agreed to be his lover he'd get her free. But she didn't dare take this offer up, as her own husband is in the SS and she is afraid of him. As Mariechen was telling this story, the little 'Russian', Frau Sch., interrupted. She said she had had a similar experience. When her fingerprints and photograph were being

85

taken at the police station she was left alone with one officer, who was friendly, talked to her for a long time, and stroked her. Frau Sch., starved of tenderness, acquiesced in this for a while, but when the policeman tried to kiss her and made his intentions quite plain the whole affair began to annoy her and she threatened to bring charges against him. He let her alone, but said she would be wise not to try it, since his weapons were the more dangerous and she would come off worst. Frau D., a newcomer, added a word too. She had had the same thing happen. So had four others. They decided to bring a charge against the man without delay.

This afternoon I was involved in an unpleasant scene at the factory. My arms were hurting so badly that I couldn't keep up with the packing, for all my stupid zeal. The packets piled up. I noticed that the two girls who work at the filling and sealing machines were speeding up more and more, so I said, 'Wait for me, please, I can't keep up.' And I showed them my bleeding arms. They paid no attention. I asked them again. They laughed scornfully. One of them called across: 'There you are, your ladyship, you can see how we work. You'd best learn it too.' I was vexed, since I'd never put on the airs of a 'lady' and as far as I could I'd fitted in with their manner. 'Oh what nonsense,' I said. 'But I've only been here a couple of days, how do you expect me to be able to do the work already?' They said to each other, 'We'll show her.' I stopped working and shouted (you always have to shout on account of the noise of the machines): 'What have I done to you? Why are you being so hateful?' They laughed and called: 'See how angry she is, her ladyship's getting all worked up.' The wardress came bustling across. 'What's all this row about?' The two girls yelled: 'It's R. starting a

86

quarrel. She doesn't want us to work so fast, just so's she can take care of her dainty fingers.' The wardress, taking the part of the mob immediately and on principle, shouted at me: 'What? Not work so fast? Why did you volunteer for outside work if you're too delicate to do the work?' My temper was up. 'Did I say I wouldn't work? Aren't I doing my job like everyone else? Haven't I worked my arms raw?' As I spoke a rage took hold of me and I shouted out loud: 'What kind of nonsense is all this anyway, these two packing up more than three hundred and twenty packets? What do we get out of it? Am I supposed to work my fingers to the bone so the breadcrumb barons in there can get rich quick on their war-effort breadcrumbs?' (Bread-crumb baron is what we call the owner – the phrase was coined by our quiet Frau R.; the breadcrumb baroness is the manageress, Fräulein Rst., a battleaxe who used to be a servant in the owner's household, had a child by him, and by way of reward has now been given a fine position. The breadcrumb princesses are the super-blonde daughters of the owner, who hang about in the office so that they will not have to work elsewhere.) My words were greeted with a total silence. To crown it all, a fuse went at that very moment, so that both machines ground to a halt. The manageress (the battleaxe) dashed out of her office, the four super-blondes put their heads timidly out of the door. Unperturbed, I went on shouting: 'That's right, they exploit us, they starve us, and in return I'm expected to sit still while two young chits get cheeky with me?' I thumped the table angrily. If I hadn't been so angry I'd have had to laugh at their stupid faces. The wardress, who cannot stand the battleaxe (why not? – because she has a secret hatred of everything above her, be it intellectually or through personality, position, or even nothing but money), was really on my side, since I was indirectly attacking the battleaxe, but she was against me too, because – well, on principle. She yelled: 'Keep your big mouth shut! You're inciting prisoners to revolt, that's what you're doing. Shut your trap, you common bitch.' Louder still, I shouted: 'I won't be talked to like that.' She tried to shout me down: 'This'll go to the public prosecutor, I promise you.' Suddenly calm and cool, I said, 'Fine by me,' and went back to my work. The battleaxe, intimidated, saw to the fuse and then withdrew silently to her office with the four super-blondes. The wardress joined the two quarrelsome girls and had a long and friendly talk with them. What will they hatch up against me? We'll see.—On the way home, a further incident: a pack of schoolboys crossed our path. When they saw us, they called out: 'The Polacks are coming, the Red bitches' – they spat at us and scattered into the darkness.

18 November 1944

This morning I was summoned before the governor. The wardress had reported me. The governor had me give a calm account of what happened, then said: 'Let me give you some advice. Never get into a quarrel with that riff-raff. You will always come off worst, because you're on your own and you don't have the weapons they have.' I stared at him in astonishment. I wouldn't have expected this of him. Spontaneously, I offered him my hand. He shook it, but then instantly withdrew his own; I thought it had suddenly occurred to him that I was a prisoner, but at that moment I saw that the head wardress had entered the next room. The governor went on in a completely different tone of voice: 'And see to it that it doesn't happen again, understood? I don't want to hear any more complaints or you'll be in detention.'—If I hadn't long been a socialist I'd have turned socialist today. Every Saturday the bakery stops work and we have to do the cleaning. It's very unpleasant. You have to clamber about on the huge machine-mills, take off every belt, oil all the bearings, take the machines apart and wash, grease, and reassemble them, climb down into the flour-pits and clear them out, all of them laborious, difficult jobs as far as I could see. But I noted this: the sequence of the tasks is fixed. First the ceilings and walls are swept clean while others begin to clean the floor. Then the milling equipment is cleaned, which raises a lot of dust. The freshly scrubbed floors are caked in sticky paste wherever the flour-dust settles on the damp surfaces. Then the tables and chairs are washed while the filling machines are being cleaned. This raises more dust. Then the floor is scrubbed again. Last of all, the sealing equipment is washed. This dirties the floor for a third time, and the furniture too. Meanwhile the storeroom at the back is vigorously swept out so that the dust from out there can settle everywhere at leisure. In the end it all looks just as it did in the beginning. Why not do the work in a sensible order? Because in that case there would always be half the prisoners with nothing to do, and that wouldn't do at all. Far better to have the work done three times over. The prisoners take their revenge in their own way: they dally. Frau R., who had to clean the windows today, took four and a half hours over them, and they still weren't properly clean. The work could easily be done in two hours. I was ordered to clean the two offices. At first I didn't find it at all unpleasant. I was on my own, it was warm, the steam-heating was pouring out heat so that I had to open the windows (in the prison they switch on the heating only on Sundays and even then only a little and not in all the cells, though there's already snow on the ground and it is cold). I knelt to do the cleaning, I scrubbed and brushed and was lost in thought when I noticed that one of the super-blonde girls was watching me through the window. She was watching me with an expression that plainly betrayed a concern that I might steal something. After a while she came in, felt at the table to see if it was really clean, and pointed at a corner: 'There's still dirt there.' 'Yes,' I said, 'I know. I haven't cleaned there yet.' She watched me for a while, pretending to have things to do at the desk, and then said, 'You don't clean properly. You have to apply more pressure.' I looked at her and then answered, 'Have you ever cleaned in here?' She was amazed. 'Me? Why should I do the cleaning? I have more important work to do.' 'Really?' I said. 'Is that so? Well, so have I.' She withdrew in a hurry. She didn't care for my tone. As long as I was cleaning the outer office she stayed out of sight. Frau R. passed by. She shook her head and said, 'Why on earth are you taking such pains? That's good enough for the breadcrumb bigwigs. Give it a rest.'

The inner office was so filthy that I was hard put to manage. Another of the super-blonde girls, the youngest, was leaning against the safe reading a newspaper. She was wearing wonderful silk stockings and an expensive woollen dress under her white coat. Her finger-nails were varnished red and she had a lot of rings on her fingers and a thick gold bangle. Her long hair was curled. I took a look in the mirror. I look like an old, lean, careworn charwoman. There were brown coffee stains on the tables. In one corner there was an electric kettle, with a coffee-pot next to it and five cups, and a basket containing a jar of honey, a few fresh rolls, and a number of small tins. There was a smell of real coffee. Scattered on the floor were crumbs from rolls, sausage skins, a whole slice of longlife wurst, a few nuts, and a number of apples bitten into. I was scarcely able to resist the temptation to eat the wurst; I was terribly hungry. A drawer was open, full of apples, small, ripe, sweet apples. The dog came in, went to the drawer, and took out a couple of apples. I said to the blonde girl, 'Watch out, the dog's at the apples.' She replied in a bored voice, 'They're his to play with.' I let out a staggered 'Oh'. I thought of an incident this morning: on our way to the bakery there is an apple tree in a garden. There are fourteen shrivelled, forgotten apples on it – we've counted them. This morning, three of them were in the street in the dirt, in a puddle. We dived on them. Those that succeeded in grabbing an apple promptly bit blissfully into it, without pausing to clean it off. The apples were sour and frozen cold, but it was something fresh and green; something precious in our diet of potatoes and cabbage.—Also, I thought of the incident in the dye works. In the factory courtyard there is an apple tree. The apples had been forgotten and were left unpicked. The prisoners were in the courtyard twice a day, for their break, and could see the apples. They asked L., their wardress, to ask the owner if they could shake down the apples that were going rotten on the tree, but she said it was out of the question. Why? Well, it was simply not possible, one day the owner would get round to picking them. The prisoners waited. At times an apple would fall from the tree – the owner hadn't a thought in the world of picking them. There is a big orchard right next to his house. One day, last week, he finally told the prisoners, 'You can give the tree a shaking-down.' They eagerly did so. The apples had gone rotten.—When I had cleaned half the office, on my knees of course, the battleaxe turned up and stomped straight across the wet floor in her dirty shoes. I retreated into a corner. It was the corner with the dog's basket. The dog leapt at me and tried to bite me. I defended myself and kicked it. The super-blonde gave an outraged shriek. 'What do you think you're doing, kicking the dog? Come here, darling. That nasty woman's going to beat you, poor doggie.' She took it in her arms and began to feed it rolls and wurst. But it only ate the wurst, and only after first sniffing it suspiciously. 'Oh,' sighed the blonde girl, 'don't you like it? Are you so full, dear darling?' She tossed the licked-at roll into the wastepaper basket. I went out for a moment, to tell the story to Frau R., who was just cleaning the glass doors of the office. She laughed: 'Don't tell me you're getting hot under the collar about that! Beginner! Just you wait, in two years things will look rather different. Patience, patience. These people will soon see what socialism's like. Or even communism.' The battleaxe must have listened in on the tail-end of this talk, because there she was at the door, beetroot-red and breathing heavily, when I entered; but she didn't dare say anything. I laughed at her brazenly. She went away. The super-blonde sneered, 'Well, when'll you finally have this done?' I said, 'Oh, I can work faster if you order me to,' gave the floor a single wipe round with the dripping wet rag, and walked out. Frau R. nearly died laughing. With this one deed I seem to have won over her cool heart. We withdrew into a corner, ate a piece of white bread that she had just stolen when she fetched water from the bakery, and chatted. Frau R. is a lawyer's wife, about forty, with one son and one daughter. Her son is a soldier. She is going to tell me the story of how she came to be in prison over the next few days.

In the end there was one further flap: a brush was missing. The battleaxe sped hither and thither in quest. 'Where's my brush?' We had to help search. The wardress ranted on at all and sundry. She yelled at the battleaxe, 'You just can't be keeping an eye on every one of them, it's not my responsibility, it's nothing to do with me.' And to us, 'You idle sluts, sluts is what you are. Look after the stuff, will you? You wait, I'll have you searched if the brush doesn't turn up of its own accord.' I thought this was a bad joke, but then we really did have to line up and the wardress felt us over, in front of the battleaxe's eyes. Nothing. In the end the brush was found in the courtyard. The bakers had borrowed it. It was a quite ordinary, cheap scrubbing brush.

This afternoon we were allowed to take a bath, or rather, to shower down in the cellar. It was wonderful. I washed my hair and afterwards used a pair of scissors R. stole from the sewing cell to trim my nails. I almost felt civilised. But we were hardly done when we all had to get into the courtyard to unload peat. It didn't take long, but it was bitterly cold and we were all terribly frozen after the hot shower. And we got full of dust again too. You could put together a catalogue of exemplary nonsenses and absurdities here. Plainly it's considered impossible that prisoners should suffer as much from the cold as the free. We seem to be a less developed species of humankind.

Sunday. This morning I was in the kitchen again, to peel vegetables. This time it was a tubful of turnips. I had resolved not to do any work, but then I thought it over, as the work does have to be done by somebody, and began peeling. After a while A. the cook turned up. I gave her a sly smile and said, 'Say, Frau A., I'm so awfully hungry. You wouldn't have a piece of bread for me, would you?' She snapped: 'No, where would we be if we started handing out bread? I'm under strict orders not to give anything away.' 'Ah,' said I, 'how nice that you're so conscientious, Frau A. Excellent. And I suppose you're not allowed to hand out any of the meat that's meant for prisoners either?' 'No,' she said, 'what d'you expect.' I went on in a confidential way, 'I bet you're a political prisoner too, aren't you?' She gave me an even more vexed look, but as she was occupied for the moment, cutting up onions for the officers' potato salad, she couldn't very well run away. She shrugged. 'Me? No, I'm here on account of a silly little blunder I made.' 'Is that right?' I said with fake innocence. 'A Frenchman, I suppose?' (She is forty-five.) She gave vent to an infuriated exclamation. The others began to listen in, grinning. One of them was Frau Sch., the saucy woman from Bremen. She gave my calf an applauding prod with her clog. I went on, 'But I'm sure they did you just as much of an injustice as they did me. You were denounced, I bet.' Frau Sch. couldn't contain herself. 'A., you can tell us about your little blunder,' she exclaimed, 'no harm done. How many hundredweight of butter did you sell off under the counter, eh, you business genius you?' To me she said, 'She's in for political reasons.

94

She harmed the Nazi party, to be exact the kids in NSV keeping. She's a poor political victim.' A. went out without a word. We laughed out loud. When the wardress came at midday to fetch us, A. said, 'See if you can send me a different lot next time. These today didn't get a thing done. They should have peeled another tubful of potatoes but all they managed were the turnips.' Frau Sch. said, 'Oho, we were getting a bit too near the bone for comfort, were we, A.?'—As we were going up the stairs I saw the little Chinese behind the bars again, standing there with his sad expression. He said softly, 'Bread.' I didn't have any. I shall see that I bring him some white bread.

In the afternoon we were suddenly given books to read, each of us got one. Someone or other had predetermined who would get which book. I'd be interested in the method of selection. The fat landlady threw Mörike's poems clear across the bed with a curse. Käthe, the sixteen-year-old, got Tolstoy's *Resurrection* and shoved it under her mattress with a yawn. She preferred to get some sleep. The SS woman, with half a stab at aptness, was given Gustav Freytag's *Ahnen*. Rosi had an anthology of consolation written by a Jesuit. Putting on a preacher's voice, she read us sentences from it, such as, 'Eschew gluttony and excess, the roots of many evils. Be thankful for poverty, for it paves the way to Heaven. Blessed are the poor. Leave the wealthy their riches, which the rust and moths will consume. You who are poor have chosen the better part. Blessed are ye . . .'—'What rubbish!' R. cried out, and flung the book into the corner. I was reminded vividly of something Rilke wrote in his *Book of Hours*: 'Poverty is a great radiance from within.'—As for myself, I'd been given an illustrated volume, *Denn wir fahren gegen*

*Engeland.** Just the thing for me. I threw it into a corner too. For a while we sat on our bunks grumbling, then, to warm up, we played blind man's buff, but in the process we spilt a bucket of water and made so much noise that the wardress came to the cell. After that we lolled on our bunks again, rather muted. Most went to sleep fairly soon. I slid Tolstoy's *Resurrection* out from under Käthe's mattress – she was snoring loudly – and began to leaf through it. Someone had underlined passages in red and noted comments in the margin. All the passages that speak of the injustice of the legal system, of corruption, and of tyranny had been heavily underlined. Frequently the comments read, 'Dreadful. Just like the Third Reich. Just like Hitler. The world will always remain as stupid, bad and base as ever.'—I noticed in passing that I'd forgotten how to read. It tired me, I forgot what was on the previous page, I was absent, and a good deal of it I scarcely understood. Now I understand why the prisoners feel no need at all of reading matter. I shall have to be very careful not to end up as dulled as they.

20 November 1944

Today I learnt Frau R.'s story. She told it me while we were walking up and down in the bakery's cramped black coalyard during a break from work. Listening to her, I quite forgot it was snowing and raining. Frau R.'s brother is a minister, a high-up Nazi. From the time they were children he couldn't stand his sister. When she came into a

* Also the title of a First World War song, which became popular again under the Nazis, meaning roughly 'we are on our way to fight England'. (Translator)

large inheritance after the death of their parents, he tried to contest the will. He lost his case. Frau R. married. After only a few years she realised that her husband was involved in shady dealing. She separated from him. Her husband joined forces with her brother, as did her daughter later on. From then on her husband and brother, but particularly her brother, were out to harm her in any way that was possible. And so one day her brother reported her for a currency offence. The affair was cleared up; Frau R. was innocent. From that day forth he hated her so much he could have murdered her. Quite literally. When he became a minister he naturally had her in his power. But she had grown cautious and saw that she gave him no chances. Some years before, her husband together with her brother and a number of accomplices from F. and T. had run a big currency racket. Frau R. was a witness to this – they hadn't rendered her harmless in time. And now it was high time that they did so. Frau R. was suddenly summoned to appear before a state doctor. Astonished and unsuspecting, she went. This official doctor was of course a big Nazi too. Frau R. told me this about her visit to him: the moment she entered the room, he took a sharp look at her, walked straight up to her without taking his eyes off her, and said, 'You're seriously ill. You have a dangerous goitre. Your glands aren't working. You'll have to be operated on.' For a moment Frau R. was stunned. Then she recalled that a friend had experienced the same thing. The doctor had diagnosed a dangerous glandular ailment and, in the face of all her resistance, had had her taken to hospital for an operation. There she had died, suddenly, without ever having had any complaints before. She had been a fierce opponent of National Socialism. So when this doctor tried to influence Frau R. in this

97

very way, she was forearmed. She laughed in his face and said, 'No, I'm not ill, I know that as well as you do.' The doctor, unwaveringly keeping his eyes on her, came closer and continued, 'I can see that you already have all the signs of advanced sickness. My dear lady, if you aren't operated on with all speed you'll be dead in less than a week.' Frau R. said coldly, 'Don't trouble any further, doctor. My brother and minister won't be getting rid of me quite so fast and so easily. I am still completely alive, thank God, alive enough to keep an eye on the doings of people like Minister R., the mayor of F., Sch. the timber dealer, public prosecutor G., and other personalities of a like kind. Tell my brother the minister that the time to gas me hasn't yet come. Goodbye.' He stared at her in amazement without making any attempt to hold her back. Before she left the room he called out, 'You didn't say Heil Hitler when you came in.' Frau R. gave a loud laugh, but she was in no laughing mood – she knew that now a life-and-death struggle had begun. Before long she was summonsed to court. She was charged with having slandered public prosecutor G. In answering the charge she declared, 'As long as people like public prosecutor G. have the law in their hands there will continue to be injustice. I'd like to have it recorded that public prosecutor G. was mixed up in a currency racket. I hereby request an investigation. I am a witness.' Her statement was ignored but she was given three months for slander. She was offered remission of the sentence on condition that she withdrew her slanderous remarks. No, she told them, she couldn't do that. She'd rather spend a whole year in prison. She was to begin serving her sentence two months later. In the mean time she was under Gestapo surveillance. They were hoping she would furnish them some pretext for putting her into a concentration camp. But she was on her guard. Meanwhile she wrote a letter to the *Reichsgerichtshof*, repeating her charges against the court at T. and particularly public prosecutor G. She got no reply. When four weeks had passed she wrote again, and again received no reply. Of course she will never get one. So now she is serving her three months, silent, embittered, proud. Z., the former bank manager, calls her our proud and silent sufferer. Frau R. told me more besides, but I have forgotten a lot. When the break was over and, still chatting away in eager undertones, we made for our machines, the wardress said snidely, 'So what important matters do you have to discuss, eh, that's what I'd like to know. Two kindred souls good and proper. Political blah-blah-blah and nothing but. You two'll talk yourselves into a noose, just you wait.' I called back cockily, 'That's right, Fräulein H., and if you're in need of any enlightenment yourself we'll gladly oblige.' She said, 'Just you go ahead thinking I'm proper stupid. I know more than you do.' In fact she knows nothing at all. In a sudden fit of bragging she told me she had worked in a chemical laboratory and had an excellent position, she'd seen a good deal of the world and had been to high school. But in reality, as Frau M. told me in the sewing cell, she was a servant girl and nothing more, and was delighted to be earning such good pay now as an assistant wardress in the prison. A funny world. Why do people always want to be more than they are? Is it somehow shameful to be a worker? Where does this warp in awareness of oneself originate? Oh, this petit bourgeois world!—When we collected our tin plates today I noticed that A., the cook, who does the doling out, gave me a particularly battered plate, and three of my four jacket potatoes were black. I didn't immediately conclude that this might be malice, but this evening I find it's the same again. The worst plate with the least food – that is her revenge.

An exciting evening. In the morning the SS woman, who had served her sentence, was released. She promised to visit us at the bakery in the late afternoon and bring us rolls and nuts. Yesterday evening she sat on Rosi and Anni's bed for a long time, celebrating her farewell, so she said. They were whispering eagerly and excitedly. I couldn't catch a word of it, and didn't especially try to, either. All day I was aware of a singular restlessness in Rosi and Anni. They claimed to have diarrhoea and kept running to the toilet every few moments. As it is out in the courtyard and we are not allowed out except under supervision, Fräulein H. had to go with them every time. It was very cold and windy outside, and the two of them took longer every time, so that at last Fräulein H. tired of the game and stopped accompanying them. The big gates onto the street are well locked up so there is no danger that anyone could escape that way, anyway. When we were already busy clearing up, the SS woman suddenly appeared. She was in civilian clothes, very elegant, her hair freshly crimped, in a word 'quite the toff', as we could see. Fräulein H. exclaimed, 'But A., you're not allowed access to the prisoners, you know that very well.' But A. was able, as she retreated towards the door, to start up a conversation with Fräulein H., while distributing rolls and nuts to us, which was also forbidden. In the end,

Fräulein H. shoved her out the door with a laugh, and we finished what we were doing and got ready to go home. Two prisoners were missing: Rosi and Anni. We waited patiently, since we're never in any hurry to return to the prison. But at length the wardress lost her patience. She shouted and ranted, and then began to call and look for them. Nothing. The factory lights had been switched off. The bakery was deserted. Now Fräulein H. started to grow suspicious. She took up a position by the street gate and ordered us to search. Neither of them was anywhere to be found. There could no longer be any doubt about it, they'd made good their escape. Fräulein H. was in a rage. For her, a couple of hundred marks were at stake, as she has to pay a fine if a prisoner escapes. The battleaxe came up yapping and excited. A big tumultuous carry-on. The prison was phoned and the police station notified. A policeman came to collect us. It was so dark you could not see your hand in front of your face. It must have been so easy for the two of them to get away. I envied them their courage and their stupidity. On the way home I remembered the evening before, and suddenly their whole arrangement was crystal clear to me. The plan had been worked out in detail with the SS woman. She was to come and leave the street gate ajar till the two of them left the toilet, where they were pretending to have diarrhoea, and then keep the wardress occupied till they had both succeeded in getting away. Neatly thought out. There was little risk for the SS woman. No one could prove she was involved in the plan.—We were summoned before the governor. With a threatening voice and pale face he said, 'If any one of you knows anything about this escape and fails to report it, she'll get four weeks' detention if I find out. So think it over. I'll give you ten minutes.' He scrutinised us closely. Uneasy silence. To show a little goodwill on our part I said, 'I was struck by their nervousness all day.' Even as I uttered the words I was annoyed at myself. What business was it of mine, and why was I speaking out against the two of them? We were sent to the cells. The whole prison was in a state of alarm. We were still at our meal when we heard the voice of the head wardress and the sobbing of the two escapees. They had already been caught. They passed by our cells. A few minutes later, triumphant and rubbing her hands, Fräulein H. came in to us and told us brimful of *Schadenfreude* that she herself had gone into town with the governor, both of them armed with revolvers. In the dark they had come across a young couple, a man and a woman. The woman asked the way to F. Her voice sounded familiar. She shone her torch into her face and saw it was Rosi. The young man was Anni. The two of them bit and scratched and fought, but in the end they came along, in tears. They had stolen dresses, underwear and money from a friend's flat and were hoping to make good a getaway. How stupidly they went about the whole affair. I am now enthusiastically occupied in thinking up an escape plan with better chances of success. One would need to have a car waiting outside the factory in the evening – in the dark, and with a false numberplate. I leap into the car, slam the door shut, and I'm away. There's civilian clothing for me in the car. I drive at eighty miles an hour. Forged passport, all my papers in order. We drive to Munich. In the bombed city I go underground. The only question is, where do I get the car? Who would risk driving it for me? Or, better still, K. drives a car up to the prison. He has a Gestapo identity card and takes me away to a hearing in Munich.—What common sense I have left tells me how idiotic all this is, as long as my children are not yet in safety. K., who is politically suspect, would immediately be arrested as an accomplice. Then what? No, I shall have to stay here. My one hope is the approach of both fronts. Who will win the race? The Russians, approaching from Vienna, or the Americans, from Colmar?

22 November 1944

Today I had my hearing – at last – here in this building, in the office. Magistrate K., a lean, tall man with spectacles, along with a secretary at the typewriter; I instantly remembered that the prisoners had described him as cynical, they told me he buttered you up and got all kinds of confessions out of you. At first I felt a certain unease, but that was soon dispelled by my concentration on repeating the statements I had made at my first interrogation word for word, without being tempted into even the slightest contradiction or variation. The magistrate looked at me closely and, as the girls had said, 'cynically', now and then smiled ironically, and then said, 'That's all well and good, but do you mean to say the witness made the whole thing up?' I resisted the temptation to embark on any new defence of my statements, and shrugged my shoulders and said, 'Your honour, all I know is what I've already said twice over. I have already explained Herr G.'s motives for denouncing me. Why Frau G., my friend, should have denounced me, I don't know. The betrayal of our friendship hurts me more than anything else.' The magistrate eyed me with interest. I could see that at that moment some change occurred in him. He leafed through the files once more and came up with the one sentence of them all that was best suited to prove the seeming absurdity of the charge. 'You supposedly said it was quite right if our children were taken away from us and raised in state homes, because we are not capable of bringing children up properly.' I had put it a lot more pointedly, I remember it well. But at that moment I put on a smile of disbelief. The magistrate said, 'You have children of your own, haven't you?' I can't say if it was really the thought of my children or the pent-up tension of an hour and a half's hearing or indeed some instinctual calculation, but I wept, or rather, to be exact, a couple of tears trickled down my face. I was vexed, but understood darkly that this was precisely the thing to do. The magistrate scrutinised me and then said, 'In my opinion it is nonsense that a mother should say such a thing.' He went on to quote one or two further exculpating sentences, things which G. had got wrong in her stupidity, and in so doing practically fed me the answers. I dimly grasped that he was trying to help me but couldn't quite believe it. When at last the questioning was finished, he asked, 'Now what would you prefer, to be transferred to our custody or remain in police custody?' I gaped, uncomprehending. I said, 'Your honour, if I'm to remain in custody it's all the same to me whose custody it is, yours or the police, and whether it's this prison or some other gaol. Doing without your freedom is bad enough either way.' He smiled. Then he dictated: 'There are no pressing grounds to suspect sedition and high treason. A warrant for arrest will not be required.' I couldn't believe my ears. At that moment I nearly fainted. Did it mean freedom? I looked at him expectantly. He stood up and said, 'The hearing is closed.' I was waiting trembling for him to say, 'You can go home.' But he said, 'You will be hearing more in due course.' He went. All day I waited to be released. In the afternoon my lawyer came, beaming: 'You got through the hearing beautifully. The magistrate is optimistic. I've little doubt we'll have you free soon.' When, radiant, I told everything to Frau R., she replied: 'I hope it goes well for you. But don't have any illusions. Your case will be put before the Gestapo again now. And you can imagine what that means.' She is right. It is better to be prepared for the worst. Nonetheless, the magistrate's decision is like a gap opened up in the dark, through which I can breathe air and see a glimmer of freedom.

23 November 1944

Another alarm this morning at four. Getting dressed at the drop of a hat, without a light, and downstairs again to the hall. I sat near Betty, the girl who was in Auschwitz. 'Darling, good to see you again at last,' she exclaimed, and pulled half a cigarette out of her pocket: 'There, as promised. It's all I have.' I gave her an apple, and we huddled close for warmth. But she is so nervous and crazy that I cannot take being close to her. She is getting thinner and thinner. She said that last Saturday they were supposed to be taking her to M., in transit to a concentration camp, but the route had been bombed.—She drew my attention to a very pretty, pale, black-haired girl who had never particularly struck me though I knew she had been in solitary confinement for six weeks, knitting socks. Her eyes were red-rimmed and she looked wretched. Betty whispered, or rather she thought she was whispering: 'She's got syphilis.' The girl turned away. I said, 'I don't believe it. How can you just say that, Betty?' 'Go on,' she said, 'you can see it. And anyway she would have been out of solitary long ago if she hadn't.' Afterwards, as we were going up, I asked Frau M., and she said yes, unfortunately it was true, and it was a scandal that she hadn't been moved. In fact she was extremely syphilitic. But nevertheless her plate and cutlery were put with ours and her bucket was emptied with ours; the prisoners who have to do this had tried refusing but without success.—That would be the last straw, being infected here. And also it's a pity about the delightful creature.—Today we were all shifted about to new quarters. Our cell has almost completely new people in it. Helena the Pole has been released, the two who tried to escape, Rosi and Anni, are in detention, on bread and water in a totally dark cell; these three have been replaced by Frau K., Mariechen and Resi, the deserter's girl, with whom I already shared cell 45. They have been allotted work in the bakery too. There was also a delicate little blonde girl, a newcomer, fifteen or sixteen years old; she went about with an American internee, against the law. She lies on her bunk quite contented, with all the books we have tossed away gathered about her, and, as she reads, she sings all the modern hit songs. She has a sweet, deep voice, but there is something about the child that I don't care for. I think she is quite cunning. She looks too innocent by half and laughed far too heartily when Käthe, the fraud from the Banat, told her jokes. The jokes were pretty obscene. Everyone else was falling about laughing. At last Mariechen, who has now spent a week in the smiths' cell, told us what went on there. On evenings when they were bored 'a longing took hold of them', as Mariechen put it, that is to say they were hankering after love, or to be precise sexual pleasure. They satisfied their needs without any embarrassment, each one on her own or else in couples, just depending. They had one or two rudimentary things to help them. Their warm-up consisted either of nude dancing or messing about. I was amazed that I had never noticed anything, and still more that these girls felt the urge for such things. I'd have thought the bromide, the unseasoned, fatless food, and the lack of stimulus would put paid to it, but Mariechen put me right on that score. The girls who work in the smithy get two big slices of wurst every day at break, with a bottle of beer. Also, they work alongside men, civilian workers who put food their way but naturally expect some service in return, which is paid them – in spite of wicked Fräulein Sch.'s watchfulness – behind machines, piles of planks, in the coal cellar, or if there is no alternative hastily in the toilet. It seems they lead quite a merry life there. That is why they look far better, more looked-after, and less embittered and deserted than the rest of us, too. M. said one of them even got pregnant like that once, but the men gave her something to get rid of it.

24 November 1944

I am tired and downcast. I want to sleep.

25 November 1944

Another cleaning day at the bakery. I told Fräulein H. I would not scrub office floors any more, I couldn't see the scattered remnants of wurst and rolls, the cigarettes and apples, without stealing. She stared at me stupidly, then ordered me across to clean machines. True, the work is harder, but it is pleasanter nonetheless. Mariechen was at work where I went to clean, going at it with true dedication. As I passed her I said, loud enough for the battleaxe to hear, 'Why work yourself so hard? Don't tell me their breadcrumb lordships have made you a present of a piece of white bread.' But Mariechen, with the soul of the born servant-girl, cannot do anything but obey and carry out her duty blindly. People like her never learn to rebel out of rational considerations.

This afternoon Fräulein B. came and asked if anyone wanted to see the Catholic prison chaplain. I was astonished. He had never come before. Nor had we ever had any kind of service in the little chapel.

I asked to see the chaplain, since it seemed a pleasant prospect to talk for once to a free human being, maybe an intellectual. Käthe asked to go too. I said: 'But you're Protestant, aren't you? And anyway, are you thinking of turning pious?' As we were going up the stairs she whispered to me, 'No, I want him to do something for me. I want him to smuggle a letter out for me.' A very long queue of prisoners were waiting in the hall in front of the chapel. I was surprised. Sch. the woman from Bremen, Mariechen, the two infanticides, the mayor's daughter from the kitchen, and the two F. sisters, older farm girls who had both had one and the same lover, a handsome Serb – they were all there, and the short fat woman from R. too, the one with the frightful rash on her hands and arms, who is so greedy she would rather let all the food she has received go bad than give any of it away. Käthe, who was in the same cell as her before, said she had been in custody for eight months now, for hoarding three hundredweight of fat, four hundred eggs, and several hundredweight of flour, not for black-marketeering but just for herself and her daughter. But when she got up every morning she cried and sighed, 'Yet another day in prison. What misery! What wretchedness! Me, a poor innocent widow, in prison. What misery . . .'

In a word, it was a curious and colourful crowd that was gathered in front of the chapel door. Almost all of them had prayer books. At that moment I realised for the first time that we were supposed to be going to confession. Fine. At the end only Käthe, Frau Sch. the woman from Bremen, and myself still remained. Frau Sch. is a protestant. She grinned when I asked her what she was after. 'Oh, all I want's to unpack my heart a bit.' I questioned this. She said she wanted to ask the priest to visit her husband, who wanted a divorce because the food coupons she had forged had landed her in prison. I had a letter in my pocket too, which I wanted him to smuggle out for me, and which would give my friends, Doctor Sch.'s family, uncensored news of me. As we were still standing waiting, the head wardress came up, gaped at us, and growled in a sneering tone, 'Off to confess, are you? I like that. You're after the priest, that's what. Don't think I don't know, you so-and-sos.' (So-and-sos means much the same as whores.) And of course I got in a temper again (when will I learn to ignore her?) and shouted: 'I won't have that. What right do you have to attack us like this? If we have permission to go to confession we don't want to have stupid remarks made at us while we're about it.' All she said was: 'Cheeky beggar, this one. Just wait.' (She always speaks to me in the third person.)

The dusky light in the hall, which was far warmer than our cells, the stand with leafy plants outside the officers' rooms, the big window with its view over the snowy garden and the violet shadows of the mountains beyond, the deep silence – all of this put me in a solemn frame of mind, and childhood memories came to mind: above all, the long passages in the monastery at W., and the piety of the little girl I once was. I went to confession. Everything went well, but when in closing the priest said, 'And when one day you return home to your life of womanly fulfilment . . .' I felt vexed. There was some tone in it, some inflexion, that irritated me deeply. You become so sensitive to genuine and false notes here. Afterwards I waited on, to talk to him in private. He is a short, dark, good-looking man. When I asked him to smuggle the letter out for me, he squirmed and tried to get out of it. I told him bluntly that I knew he had already smuggled letters out. He denied it. But I know it for certain. So I pressed him. In the end he promised to take the letter. He accepted Käthe's letter to her parents immediately – why this double standard? I did not feel happy about the encounter. It may be that prisoners who have committed real crimes find considerable comfort in confessing. It probably does the prisoners good to have someone paying attention to them in a slightly more caring way. And for many it is also the well-loved habit of many years and a source of solace. But for some the incentive is a different one. As I went down I met the short, rotund cook, H., at the grille where we had to wait. She is still in despair. She had been to confession as well. She whispered, 'He's handsome, the priest. If I have to stay in here for many months before . . .' I didn't understand what she meant. 'What then?' She smiled: 'He's a man.' I stared at her (I am a lot stupider than most in here). She burst out laughing. 'Don't you get me? A little loving . . . and even if it's only one-sided it's nice and it comforts you.' I am convinced she really will give it a try. It is far less reprehensible than it sounds. Quite apart from the fact that it will presumably remain no more than a dream, a case like this is not primarily the result of immorality but rather of the instinct for survival, for self-preservation. In here, you look for something or other, some focal point where you can gather up whatever energy, feeling, and thought that has not been drained out of you by the perpetual triste, crude, evil sameness. That point is what gives you your life. Not everyone finds it in something of the mind. I have not the slightest reason to feel superior. In my darkest hours, when all wisdom fails, I comfort myself with the thought that one day the Nazis will sit here, in these same walls. Is this feeling, which at such moments is nothing but hatred, so very high? Sometimes in here I confront myself as I have never done before. I see myself with all my base instincts, with false, lying, romantic notions of honour, morality, class-consciousness and all the beautiful, conventional ideas one acquires. In the end all that is left is the animal, wanting to eat and sleep, afraid of being beaten, yearning for freedom. In our lives outside we simply disguise all of that with a lot of words.

26 November 1944

Sunday. In the morning we had to unload two truckfuls of shoes. The shoes had been accumulated some time or other, for soldiers or whatever. At all events they are to be recycled for the materials. They had been covered in snow and were frozen. The work was unpleasant. But it was enjoyable all the same. There were several hundred pairs: slippers, gym-shoes, children's shoes, dancing slippers, wedding shoes. All ragged and tattered. Many of the prisoners took the best shoes and hid them under their jackets, to use as slippers. I began to search out the prettiest dancing shoes and try them on. Fräulein H., the prison dachshund, was in a good mood and let us be for a while. We put all the dancing shoes on a snowed-over wall: gold, silver, brocade, silk, all with worn-down heels, torn buckles, big holes. Worn out from dancing. A strange sight, all this worn and tattered glory in the middle of the prison yard. Like in a fairy-tale.

In the afternoon we were all very bored. We were in a dismal frame of mind. It was snowing. We were homesick and hungry and had no books. Then I remembered an old party game, a kind of ouija with a glass. We tore off small scraps of toilet paper, wrote one letter of the alphabet on each, and placed them on the table around an upturned tooth-glass. Then Frau H., Rosi and I placed our finger-tips on it and the glass really did start to move. The girls were greatly amazed. I asked questions, and the glass replied by indicating letters that spelled out whole words and sentences. Some of the girls were confused and awe-struck, the others thought it nonsense and a fraud, till I began to ask the 'spirit' about facts in the private lives of the other prisoners, which were unknown to me, and always got the right answer. At this of course we all asked the date of our release. To me, the spirit replied, 'Before Easter.' To Frau H.: 'Soon after that.' To the rest: 'When the war ends.' We asked when the war would be over. 'Soon.' I did not dare put political questions of a more precise nature, since Mariechen is very gossipy and Käthe unpredictable. Among other things, the glass said that after the war was over we would all go through a period of terrible poverty. As to who would liberate us here, it might be a Russian. When I finally asked the spirit his name, he replied, 'I am H.G.' An old friend of mine who died a long time ago. He said: 'I am only here on your account; the rest are a nuisance. Ask more things that you want to know another time when there are not so many.' I said nothing of this to those who were not reading along. —Since the afternoon they have been sitting at the table without a break, asking, asking, asking. I am lying on my bunk, resting.

Scarcely had I thought that for once I really did have some peace but Frau H., the one with heart trouble, sat on my bed. She was having a particularly bad day. Her heart was giving her pain, she had no medicine, she was worrying about her son in Norway, and in a word she was in despair. It is a despair one only finds here in prison: a vague misery, staring out into a desolate, dark waste. One only wants to die. If anyone is in this mood here, it is not good to leave her alone. So Frau H. fled across to me. She told me how she came to be arrested. She was living in with some revolting people who would have liked to get her out of the flat. One day they hit on the best way and denounced her for listening in to forbidden broadcasts. To be exact, they claimed that in winter 1941 Frau H. listened to the Swiss station every morning at seven. That is her charge. Now of course 1941 is already well behind us, for one thing, and for another Frau H. says she is hard of hearing and for that reason was never able to listen to banned stations because it was too risky; she said she had only listened to the Swiss station a time or two so that – as she'd told the people at the time – she would have some clear factual news to counter the wild rumours of the other foreign stations with. I laughed at her. It wasn't her business to propagandise for Hitler; for all her distress I could not help telling her that now she was in prison for nothing but her own stupidity, her own daft blunder. That was her thanks for loving her Führer. She even claimed that once she indirectly saved his life by thwarting assassination preparations in a train. I said, 'You idiot.' 'Yes,' she said, 'you're right, I was an idiot. But there really isn't any other man to touch the Führer.' 'In that case,' I said, 'you'd best sit out your term for love of him, hadn't you? You've already suffered for him once, four months inside Hohensalzburg before 1938.' She said softly, 'I really was an idiot, you're quite right.' But I am convinced her heart still beats for Hitler. And if one day he dies or is strung up, she will be one of the old women weeping real tears for him, although he has landed her in prison twice, hounded her only son off to war and perhaps already taken him from 'her, and will take from her the pension she gets on her son's account. There is never any end to stupidity, never.

27 November 1944

Today was a day of bad luck at the bakery. First a heavy lid fell on Käthe's head and nearly knocked her out, then I cut the middle finger of my left hand deeply on a rusty machine-part. It was bandaged and I still had to go on working; I don't think I have written yet that I am working at a sealing machine now; I have overcome my great fear of machines I don't know but have to use; and am more skilful at it than I thought. But the third misfortune was the worst: a very heavy, stout iron chain fell on the head of Resi, a strapping farmgirl who works at the drying oven. She fell to the floor, unable to speak; she had not fainted but was concussed. A doctor should have been phoned for immediately. But that, of course, did not happen. Resi was laid on an old sack in a corner, one or two cold compresses were applied, and there she was left until we returned to the prison at midday. She tottered along, propped up between two of us. She was looking around wildly and still couldn't speak. At lunchtime she was sick. I told Fräulein H. that Resi was seriously concussed. She pooh-poohed the idea: 'It won't be that bad. We've seen it all. In prison they make a mountain out of every molehill.' Resi was taken to her cell and remained lying there. When we returned in the evening she was delirious and had a temperature. Fräulein H. told the governor. By chance I heard the exchange as I was going down with our empty bowls:

H.: One of them got a chain on the head at the bakery.
G.: Well?
H.: I don't think it's serious but she may be slightly concussed.
G.: Rubbish, the prisoners just play-act. As we well know. Give her cold compresses and something to help her sleep. She'll be fine tomorrow.
H.: But I won't be held responsible.
G.: Nonsense. Responsible! I'll tell the doctor, so it'll all be perfectly correct. Then if he wants to come it's his affair. The creatures play up accidents like this superbly.

Well, the doctor has not been yet. I just went to empty the bucket and looked in at Resi's cell. Resi is deathly pale. She recognises no one, stays lying in a contorted, cramped position, and groans. She doesn't talk or eat and rolls her eyes. Is she putting it on? I do not think so. I just heard that our appalling wardress Sch., who beat the inmates and called us bolsheviks, has been transferred by way of disciplinary action. The population took a hand, and Sch. has been put to work in the munitions factory. Great feelings of triumph among us all. On top of everything, the chief wardress is ill with some kidney complaint, and is to undergo an operation. We are so jubilant we go leaping about the beds chanting songs of thanksgiving.

28 November 1944

The doctor has still not been to see Resi. There has been no change in her condition. A dangerous mood of rebellion among the prisoners. When the alarm sounded, Resi was left completely alone up in her cell.

Today I overheard a conversation in the bakery. Henriette and Jeanette have had a friend for some time, a Yugoslav, a young, good-looking lad who works in the bakery during the day and at night sleeps somewhere in a camp for foreigners. Jeanette, who is seeing to the heating now in Frau B.'s stead, frequently has the chance to talk to him. The heating is in the cellar. The Yugoslav is often sent to shovel coal down there, and when he does so they get a little talk going. Jeanette steals white bread for him as he is neither able nor allowed to take anything from the bakery. In return the boy brings her cigarettes. Today I heard the two of them talking over an escape plan, which is plainly already in an advanced stage of preparation, in German, which both speak only brokenly. They have civilian clothes, money, false passports. Just a few more days, then—. In the break I whispered to Jeanette, 'Just see you do it better than Rosi and Anni.' She froze. Then she exclaimed in a haughty voice: 'What nonsense. Who said anything about it?' I said, 'You did. And far too loud. And of course I really wish you success.' Since that moment she has hated me.

As of today we are no longer allowed to our cells for the lunchtime break. All the outside workers, some forty prisoners, sit at three tables in one cell, crushed so close together that we can hardly move. The air is so bad you could cut it with a knife, from the smell of wet steaming clothes, poor food, the pervasive colour-dust the dye-workers bear with them, and our flour-dust. No one has any appetite. The meals are getting smaller and worse all the time. Vegetables boiled in water, more fluid than vegetables, and three or four potatoes with them, often still hard, that is all. Those of us who work in the bakery smuggle in as much white bread as we can and distribute it around the prison. That is the lifeline for all of us. After we have eaten we have to sit still for three-quarters of an hour, after first washing the spoons with cold water in a common bowl and cleaning the tabletops. Many lay their heads down on the table and fall asleep. Others comb their hair, one will pluck another's eyebrows, the French-women natter loudly, so interminably and fast that you cannot understand a word of it except for 'les boches' now and then; the two F. sisters, who are inside because of the Serbian lover they shared, weep; the smithy-workers tell obscene stories at their table, Käthe whimpers with tooth-ache, Frau H. tells the tale of her arrest for the hundredth time, Z. avails herself of the bucket in the corner, un-abashed and very noisily, with loud groans and splashing sounds. Frau H., the Russian and I have a more or less sensible conversation. I remembered that witty description of the characters of various peoples which ends by saying of the Germans:

> Un Allemand – un servant
> deux Allemands – une organisation
> trois Allemands – la guerre.

I noticed that everyone had been listening to me. When I called out, 'Three Germans mean war' in translation, there was total silence. Suddenly, as if the word had been given, a little revolt broke out. Everyone began to talk, rant, and complain. Every single one thinks war the worst of evils. I suppose that when the masses are in an even worse state, when this war has brought us to abject poverty, everyone will finally see that war is the greatest of idiocies and the greatest of sins. That aside, ideas are never grasped by the people. They only comprehend what is palpable. We are in a bad way in prison. We are inside because we – about three-quarters of us – have committed so-called wartime offences: love affairs with aliens, listening to prohibited radio stations, black-marketeering, forging ration coupons, taking journeys without permission, thieving out of sheer necessity, the abortion of illegitimate children conceived by foreigners, voicing anti-regime and anti-war opinions. So the war is to blame for our sitting here frozen, hungry and beaten. And so war is a bad thing.—Those who are profiting from the war (such as my one-time friend G., who denounced me, who said the war was a blessing because at last their finances were being put in order, what with her husband's good money as an officer and the continuing teacher's salary) – they of course consider the war a good thing. My God, how stupid people are.

The doctor has still not been to see Resi. She does not seem worse, but her condition is worrying. Whenever the governor or a wardress comes near, Frau Sch. says in a loud voice, 'They just let us die here. Here in prison, and all over Germany. That's how it is.' They yell at her every time but she keeps at it firmly. I told her she'd end up in a concentration camp. 'Ach,' she said, 'three years in gaol isn't much better either. At least in a camp I'll be with sensible people.'

The wound in my hand is beginning to fester. In spite of the evidence of experience I have asked to see the doctor. I can hardly work, but of course I have to. When we wash the machines I always have to reach into the greasy, filthy water with that hand. Fräulein H. says, 'It'll heal,' but the women say wounds don't heal in prison because your blood has become too poor here.

Today I was finally able to get a piece of white bread to the sad little Chinese. He thanked me with a slow bow and a smile, then turned very quickly and abruptly crammed the half loaf into his mouth. He looks ill.—At noon the alarm sounded. Today we were in a men's cell, whose occupants had been moved into a neighbouring cell while the alarm was on. We had already been in that cell twice, and pretty little Frau N. and I had been leafing through a magazine that was lying about both times. Today there was a little letter in the magazine. 'To the beautiful, black-haired woman who comes into the cell when the alarm's on.' This was nothing to do with me: I passed the letter on to the pretty woman. She read it and laughed. It was a love letter, passionate, sentimental, longing – everything a love letter should be. The writer asked her for a few lines by way of answer or he would hang himself. I advised her to indulge in a romantic love story, it will cheer us all up. This morning I went to the dentist with Käthe and Mariechen and B. the wardress. It felt strange to be sitting in my dirty, torn prison clothes next to civilised human beings all of a sudden – who all edged away from us suspiciously. Nor am I sure whether Käthe might not have lice, for instance. She is forever scratching herself. Furthermore, we all stink of dust, sweat, and dirty clothing; our hands are not clean, our nails are broken, our hair is unkempt and grey with dust. I had a powerful urge to speak my purest high German and tell Fräulein B. – who is very nice and soon to be married – all about my private work, so loudly that everyone would hear. How could I merely be another prisoner like all the rest? How stupid people are, how stupid and vain. So I kept my mouth shut, ashamed, but nonetheless noticed with satisfaction that two well-dressed men were watching me with interest. I was ashamed, but nevertheless my self-confidence had been reinforced a touch. I have a great desire to put aside all this benighted nonsense of being better than other people once and for all, and be just a human being pure and simple, and nothing but. Yes, but – once again there is a but: am I not in fact a cut above the rest? (Whether being better is due to my upbringing, my natural disposition, or my own efforts is not the point.) But am I not cleverer than the rest? Can't I see through a lot more, can't I see how things are much more clearly? Don't I think things over quietly while the rest just rant? Even here, amid filth and crudity, am I not living my own life, following the dictates of the spirit? Ach, I don't know. Often all the ideas of the equality of men and fraternity seem dreams and nothing more. The prisoners, almost without exception, are stupid, egoistic to the point of brutality, malicious, quarrelsome. The dentist, an elderly gentleman, was charming. He did not treat us like prisoners at all. He could not lavish more caring treatment on his worthiest patients. I said to Fräulein B.: 'It's a blessing for us poor wretches when somebody behaves pleasantly to us.' The dentist turned and said: 'I happen to have a particular affection for people such as yourselves.' I could have hugged him, for – even if I often preserve a distance between myself and the prisoners – in my dealings with free people I feel a total solidarity with the other prisoners.

30 November 1944

K. came. This time I was prepared because a prisoner whispered to me that there was a 'visitor's permit' for me. By that she meant a visitor who had been granted a permit to visit. But you cannot go to the office alone, instead you have to wait till a wardress fetches you. It was just lunchtime. Frl. H., who goes home for lunch at noon, was impatient and in a hurry. 'Let Frl. B. bring her in,' she called, and went. Frl. B. said, 'Won't be a moment,' and disappeared. There I stood in the hall with my dish of potatoes. Whenever the office door opened I could see K. sitting there. He saw me, I saw him, and time after time the door was shut between us, and still Frl. B. didn't come. Our precious time was slipping by. I ate a potato, which was rotten. Then I sat down on the floor and stared at the door behind which K. was waiting. A. the cook gave me a scornful look. After twenty minutes had passed, Frl. B. raced by. I said in a beseeching tone, 'Frl. B., my visitor is waiting.' She shouted: 'Yes, yes, just a moment,' and vanished once again. I was trembling with impatience. At last the governor turned up. I asked him to let me in. He hesitated, then did so. For a full fifteen minutes I was alone with K., with no one listening except Z. the bank manager, who likes me. Every minute was exquisite. K. hastily whispered the political news. They say Hungary has capitulated but only partly, that is to say another fascist government has been installed. Progress is being made, but slowly, desperately slowly; the whole fabric is rotten, arms factories are being bombed, aircraft have no fuel, but the war will by no means be over by Christmas as we prisoners imagined. Maybe Easter. Churchill said too that the war would last into the new year. K. also told me he is under Gestapo surveillance. He quickly shoved a few new papers across to me, which I hid inside my blouse. We talked over money matters and household issues. I was very composed and this time I didn't cry. But K. was horrified by my appearance, above all by the many grey hairs I now have. True, he said I looked better than last time, but I could tell from his distressed gaze that he found me ugly. When I leant against his arm I dirtied the sleeve of his coat. K. said I was still very much on top of things mentally. And so I was, in those minutes I spent with him, I was excited and worked-up, but normally I no longer am. When K. had left I was sick. Any unusual excitement triggers sickness and diarrhoea in here. K. also said I would be home for Christmas. But doubtless he was only consoling me.

Today the doctor finally saw Resi, or to be exact Resi went to see him. She was half carried, half dragged to his surgery. He said it was nothing much, quite usual, she just needed to lie for a day or so and she'd be fine. Resi can scarcely move her tongue. He gave me ointment for my finger, but conveyed quite unambiguously that he thought it superfluous in the extreme. Frl. H., the dachshund, said less out of malice than out of stupidity, 'That's right, R. is a particularly refined lady, you see, and her fingers are terribly terribly delicate.' I held my work-roughened hand with its scratches and the large, festering wound under her nose. She told me she'd had worse injuries and still gone on working.

Today we witnessed an uncomfortable scene. We were at work in the bakery. Suddenly an SS man came in, said a few words to Frl. H., and then called Mariechen. When she opened the door she let out a loud shriek. We could see another SS man standing outside, a brutal-looking youth who greeted her with an immobile, threatening expression. Frl. H., who loves a sensation, whispered, 'That is M.'s husband.' Poor Mariechen. Ten minutes later was our break. Frau R. and I watched the two of them from a distance. He was still talking at her grimly and coldly, exactly as if he were negotiating with a total stranger. She was crying, and wiped her eyes with her dirty apron. After a while he held her in his arm and spoke to her in a more friendly manner. Then he gave her a couple of rolls and left. Mariechen gaped after him, weeping, then came over to us laughing and crying. 'He wants a divorce,' she said. 'You should be pleased,' I said, 'then you'll be rid of the lout.' She sobbed again and said in good high German:

'But I love him so very much.' We laughed out loud. 'That swine? The SS man? That brutal lout? You just let him go. Didn't you say he tried to poison you, too?' In tears, she told us, 'But he was so good to me just now. He held his arm round me and gave me two rolls.' We answered, 'Isn't that something! Two whole rolls! He really took pains over that present.' We comforted her for a while. At length she exclaimed in a triumphant voice: 'Now I can love Roland just as I like, now I can marry him.' (Roland is her Frenchman.) Fine, we said, but first be free once more.—

I shall never forget that man's face. It was the face of the SS: ice-cold, totally in possession of the power and the weapons to wield it, brutal, the face of the professional killer. I advised Mariechen to tell the divorce court that he had tried to poison her. Ach, she said, nobody'll believe me anyway. No one will lift a finger against the SS. She may be right there.

These days I always have so little time to write, for at lunchtime I cannot, with all the noise in the cell where we eat, and in the evenings I am so tired that I have difficulty thinking. And anyway the girls always want to play at pushing the glass, and I have to help with that.

2 December 1944

Cleaning day. Bathing in the afternoon. Then the lawyer was there. We had to wait a long time again. Today the SS major was absent. The smith from R., who is two metres tall, said the major has been acquitted by the *Volksgerichts-hof*. Of course. What else. The five political conspirators from R. have dismal prospects. They have already been close to having a death penalty handed down once, but they had been able to find witnesses in their defence. 'The whole game's enough to make you throw up,' said the tall man. 'You'd like to shout it all in their highnesses' faces – you know what. But what's the point? The war's only got a month or so to run. I don't intend to hang.' He's right.

One thing struck me: Frau L., the youngest of the assistant wardresses, a great hulking creature whose husband was killed a few months ago and whose young child died recently, is without a doubt man-mad. Today the men were handed out their clean clothing. Usually it is a male warder that does this. She pushed forward and cried out: 'I'll do it, I'll do it.' This evening I saw her – she thought herself unobserved – trying it on with the tall man. She brushed by him very close, several times, and at last placed her hand gently on his arm. He did the same, taking the mickey. But she thought he was responding genuinely. In the end he thrust her away in disgust, but still she registered nothing. So he turned away, rudely, and yawned. When at last she left him alone he said out loud to me: 'What a stupid cow.' She heard this in going, turned, and laughed. I have never seen anyone as stupid. And this is the kind of person we have as wardress. We are at the mercy of her whim, her crude, thoughtless power. She wears size 43 shoes, has a voice like a man's, and her eyes are stupid and bulging. She is my superior. If she likes she can beat me, have me put in detention, hand out punitive tasks, be rude to me – I have no defence.

The little cook was ahead of me to see the lawyer. She came out in a rage. What was the matter? She had been reproaching him bitterly for advising her to plead guilty as the war would soon be over anyway. 'The war isn't over,' she shouted, 'and here I am with eleven months to do.'

An interlude: a scene from a little drama. A pretty

woman with a good many blonde plaits pinned up, an inn-woman from F., this side of the grille, and the other side a fat man, apparently an inn-keeper too. Both of them debating hotly and fiercely. They are quarrelling. I hear the woman hiss, 'And it's all your fault. If I hadn't had to look after you I'd never have done it. But now I don't have anyone to help me. And I shan't lift a finger for you.' The man, imploring: 'But I swear I didn't give a thing away. I don't know . . .' The woman: 'I don't want anything else to do with you. Our love is over and done with. You can forget about marrying.' The man, crushed: 'Just listen to me . . .' The woman, unsure of herself, hesitant, half turns back to him. 'Well, what do you have to say? I won't believe another word you say.' You can see how much she loves him. They fall to whispering all over again.—The woman had a Wehrmacht depot on her property and stole articles from it and sold them off. The man is involved in the affair up to the hilt.—Afterwards we exchanged a few words. She said, 'What, you're a writer? When I'm free again you'll have to write my life story. It's really interesting. A regular novel. I'll have to write it all for my grandchildren! You could earn yourself a lot of money. I pay well. I have a lot of money. Writers need money.' I told her politely that so far I had been accepting commissions from publishers rather than private people, but still: if the ban on my writing remains, it would be a source of income.—Seriously: the devil knows what we are going to live on one day. I shan't flinch from any work that is part of the labour of reconstruction, however trivial. Ach, to be able to work again, work, talk, be free! The lawyer was in a bad mood. He growled, 'Your case hasn't been going as expected. The files were sent to the district court at R. and the case ought to have been dismissed there. Today you'd long have been a free woman. But the public prosecutor there is a great Nazi and didn't dare or want to quash it. So the business is now in the hands of the *Volksgerichtshof* in Berlin. Idiotic, really. It may go on a long time. Months. I'm telling you the plain truth. No illusions.' I left feeling numbed. But now I have my composure back. The war will not last forever. A concentration camp – which is where all this is leading – will be bearable for so short a time. And maybe things will never reach that point.

3 December 1944

Sunday. The prison chaplain came again today. We had a short service and then we were able to talk to him in private. Frau H. the cook was there, of course. She had done her hair nicely and rubbed her cheeks with red paper. I laughed at her. I was the last. The chapel was almost totally dark. The chaplain offered me a seat beside him in a pew, and asked, 'Well, my dear Frau R., how are we? Have you accepted God's will? Are you at peace with God?' Vexed, I said, 'Don't give me that. I'm not in any frame of mind for religious talk. I've got quite different worries. Just tell me how far the Allies and the Russians have got. No one knows anything for certain.' Gently, he answered, 'The Allies are still far to the left of the Rhine, the Russians are in East Prussia and at the Plattensee, but apart from that I know nothing.' 'Ach,' I exclaimed, 'that's the German Wehrmacht version. But what do the foreign stations say?' 'Oh,' he said, 'I can't tell you that.' 'Oh no? Don't you listen to them? Never?' I asked, disappointed. He said, 'I have come to give comfort to your soul. Let us leave politics alone.' I shouted at him:

'What good is comfort for my soul? At the moment politics are a lot more important to me, to all of us. Politics decide when we will be free, when we will be human beings again. You don't know what we go through here. We don't need consolation, we need better food and different treatment. We need freedom, otherwise we'll just die.' He leant close to me and whispered, 'Not so loud, they may hear us.' I laughed contemptuously. I asked, 'What about my letter? Did you send it?' He took it out of his pocket. 'No, I couldn't square it with my conscience.' I made no reply, but I was so angry that I hunted about in my mind for something nasty to retort. But then, crestfallen and disappointed, he said, 'Ach, and I came today on your account, I had so much work to do but I thought, Frau R. needs me.' When he said that I felt sorry for him. I thanked him for taking the trouble and left.—Simply one more let-down, nothing more than that. The others were tirelessly shoving the glass about. They are doing the same thing in all the cells. Word has got round. When we were emptying the buckets, little Frau N. told me they had some spirit called Potemkin who said Germany would be Russian one day. The remarkable thing is that no one in that cell knows who Potemkin was, none of them has ever studied politics. Soon I shall be starting to believe in a ghost myself.

4 December 1944

Today the two blonde Frenchwomen were suddenly absent at the bakery. I supposed they had been released. No one knew anything about it. But in the evening I heard their voices as they entered the cell. Hastily, as we were emptying the buckets – awful, disgusting job that I'm sure the young girls would relieve me of, but I do it so that I experience every last thing here exactly as it is – I found out that the two of them are under detention; all day they sit in the coal cellar sewing sacks. Their friend, the Yugoslav, was caught making his escape attempt from the camp, with a bundle of civilian women's clothing and false passports. He confessed everything, presumably not voluntarily (we are familiar with their methods), and said the two sisters were his accomplices. They are out of luck with escape attempts. I feel sorry for them. So now they sit there from seven in the morning till five in the evening, without a break, in the suffocating cellar. For what? For trying to get home, for making preparations for something we would label heroic or at least brave and admirable: flight from alien tyranny, return home to the fatherland. But they are 'only' French girls, the daughters of the defeated; so into the cellar with them. Where would we be if we had the same laws for Germans and foreigners? If we treated foreigners as human beings?—The Frenchwomen hate us unreservedly, as if we prisoners were to blame. When we were eating this evening I had a scene with Hermine, a Belgian woman. We can get three or four Camelias from the wardress every four weeks. Hermine had got hers and placed them on the table as we were eating, right in front of me. I said, 'Will you please move those.' She didn't answer. I repeated what I had said. She pulled a face at me. I told her I had always felt friendly towards her but she was coming on pretty badly. I swept the Camelias from the table. The other prisoners were on my side. Hermine laid them back on the table with deliberate emphasis. Should we have got into a fight? I wondered about it, but in the end thought – why? I capitulated before the hatred in Hermine's eyes. Nobody has national pride to compare with our Frenchwomen's – they are mean little misses, mostly, but 'vive la France'. It's not a jot better than 'Deutschland über alles'. As long as we stay like this there will be no peace in the world.

By way of a pendant to yesterday's event, as it were, there was another today. A Russian woman from Rostov, Tamara, a twenty-one-year-old medical student, joined us. A hefty, powerful girl, quiet, broad, cheerful, and clever. She landed in gaol because she made a journey without the necessary papers – only a fifteen-kilometre trip. But she is Russian, and that is sufficient grounds for suspicion. She works at a dairy. I asked if she was a communist. No, she said, there weren't so very many party members. Were the rest opposed to it? Opposed? Opposed to what? She stared at me uncomprehendingly. Opposed to Stalin, I said, to communism. 'Why should we be?' she demanded ingenuously. 'We're doing fine.' Weren't they very poor? 'Poor? Not at all. We all have something to eat, somewhere to live, work to do, why should we be poor?' Her father is a cobbler. The state paid for her to go to high school and university. At present, during wartime, her parents have to contribute a proportion, about a quarter. Medical students have excellent prospects. Did they really, as we hear, live ten to a single room? No – at home they have three rooms for five people. Others have more. There are people who do not work much, and they have less. You can earn well if you work. Was she enthusiastic about Stalin and his ideas? She shrugged: 'We don't think about it. We haven't experienced anything different. It's fine the way it is. We don't want anything else.' Did she hate us Germans? Gently she shook her head. 'Only the ones that lock me up. And Hitler, of course. He ruined our country and my family and dragged me away and all he wants is war.' A pity that Tamara knows so little German and I have only three words of Russian. There is so much more that I'd like to know, and she would like to hear a lot from me too.

6 December 1944

In the night, no doubt inspired by the conversation with Tamara, I had a strange dream. I was in a big, unfamiliar city, wandering in a tangle of narrow alleys and lanes. Suddenly I was in a courtyard lined with galleries. For some time I was completely alone. Suddenly a funeral procession turned up, a great number of people, I couldn't see the coffin, but there were three women dressed in black. They weren't crying, they were almost smiling or laughing. I was perplexed and said half aloud, 'Why are you laughing if you're in mourning?' They said, 'We have been forbidden to weep, and we're not sad anyway.' When the procession had passed by, a kind of Chinese or Cossack armed as a swordsman leapt in, lunged and thrust, and shot off a revolver in all directions. I stood enthralled. It was like a dance. He shot at me too, but the bullets passed straight through me, easily, as if I had no body. Then a uniformed man came up and led me away down long passageways. Somewhere there was a bucket, a latrine bucket like in prison. I knew the bucket had to be taken somewhere and, silently and without waiting to be asked, picked it up and took it along with me, although it disgusted me. Then we were suddenly in the open and there was a steep wall of planks. The man said, 'This is where you have to go down.' Without hesitation I slid down, though I did not know where I would fetch up down below. The uniformed man was instantly at my side. Then he took me to a vast hall. In it, seated at long tables, were a great many men and women, writing. Without introducing me, the uniformed man announced, 'She passed the test.' Another man, seemingly the boss, replied, 'We'll have to determine whether she has leadership qualities.'

I have not told the others about this dream. Normally we tell each other our dreams every morning. A number of interpretations are accepted here. If you dream about vegetables or fruit you can expect something good. But you mustn't eat them in your dream, or something will be taken from you. Dreams of new hats, new clothes, new shoes mean a change. Dreams about snow are also favourable, as are those of bright, smokeless fires. Smouldering fires mean bad luck, unpleasantness, gloom, quarrels. A train journey is erotic. If you see dogs and horses in a dream it means your friends will stand by you. The night before I was interrogated I dreamt of an apple tree laden with ripe apples, and a horse. When I am free again I shall have to devote some of my life to considering dreams. If I attempt anything like thought here I am exhausted after a few minutes and my head spins. My memory is failing so badly that often I cannot remember the names of inmates. For some days my hearing has been weaker. A great many have found the same thing happening to them once they have been inside for six or seven weeks. My finger is full of pus. There is a fat blister filled with pus on it, but it isn't ready yet. Today I wanted to go to the doctor to have it lanced, but Frl. H., the dachshund, said, 'Come off it, you snivelling sissy, you should be ashamed. You can't go bothering the doctor with something like that.' Work at the machine, for which I need the first three fingers of my left hand in particular, is very difficult.—Resi is still sick, but she is feeling better. I heard that the little Chinese is badly ill, and I can't get any more bread to him.

This afternoon I realised that today is St Nicholas's. This time no one at home will be thinking of hanging a sack of nuts and apples and *lebkuchen* at the door, I suppose, or rattling chains. A couple more weeks and it will be Christmas, and I shall still be in prison.

7 December 1944

At lunch today Frau Sch. (from the smiths' table) brought a package tied in string to our table. It was adorned with a sprig of fir and looked Christmassy. 'Here,' she said, 'a late St Nicholas present, from Father Christmas.' She withdrew in mock innocence. I unwrapped it; I thought it was a little sausage. Once the outer wrapping was off an elongated thing lay revealed, tightly bound, with a look of a babe in diapers. I was astonished. What on earth was it? Suddenly everyone around me burst out in wild laughter. I hadn't the faintest idea why. Gently, they informed me of the purpose of the object. It was an artificial phallus. That is the kind of joke that gets played in prison.

This afternoon A., Mariechen's friend who has performed so many abortions (we nicknamed her the 'midwife'), was suddenly missing. Mariechen sobbed. The midwife had been released. She had got herself a woman lawyer who had obtained her release without a trial. Why?

She has eight proven abortions, in the second to fifth months, to account for. Mariechen underwent only one and she is still in gaol, with no prospects, as my lawyer said, to whom I recently described Mariechen's case. I advised her to request a lawyer who acts for the down-and-out, and she wrote the request on Sunday. But I do not believe any lawyer can accomplish anything in her case. Her husband, the SS man, does not want to see her go free. He has his reasons. And in any case the divorce proceedings have begun. My lawyer says she will lose, quite probably will even lose the child as well (she has a four-year-old girl by her husband).

8 December 1944

Odette, the girl from Versailles, has a lover – at least, the others believe he is her lover. But I think it is something different. For a week now a man has been standing at a dark corner when we come back from the bakery in the evening. He walks along with us a little way, very close to Odette, like some harmless pedestrian. For a few days the wardress didn't notice anything. He and Odette have long, whispered conversations in their rapid Versailles French. He passes her things, without attracting attention, and she slips them rapidly into her neckline. When she gets to the prison she sometimes has a great deal stuffed in her front. No one notices a thing. Yesterday I saw the man at lunchtime. He is about forty or a little older, short, fat, nimble, poorly dressed, and wears a bright red scarf about his neck. A dangerous, nasty character. I was barely able to catch a single word of their talk, whispered between their teeth. Today, at last, Frl. H. saw what was going on. She shot her mouth off and forbade the man to walk along with us. He laughed. Odette said something aloud to Frl. H., quickly and in a polite manner. It was intended to seem like an explanation, but in fact consisted of a dozen or more crude swear-words. Frl. H., of course, does not understand any French. Frau R. and I laughed ourselves silly. Frl. H. was in a rage. She went up to the man as if she was going to box his ears, but he gave her a friendly laugh. She shouted and scolded the whole way. The man said, 'Not understanding,' and went along quietly. In the end Frl. H. said she would place Odette in detention if the man didn't stop. At this, the man withdrew, with a threatening, malicious look at the wardress. Odette is so impertinent and forward that I can only admire her. But how are we Germans ever to be reconciled with France, or with Poland and other peoples, if we treat them like this now? The incidents that take place in prison here are only a handful among the thousands throughout the Reich. It is a bad seed we are sowing.

9 December 1944

There was a great uproar today. B., the fat inn-woman, was caught stealing white bread at the bakery. The battleaxe saw her shoving a piece of bread into her mouth. So she leapt at B. and snapped at her – 'Hand that bread over right away!' – and B. opened her mouth and showed her the chewed-up bread clinging to her teeth. The battle-axe ran across to Frl. H. 'The prisoners are stealing bread again.' Frl. H., who is always in a rebellious mood as far as the battleaxe is concerned, said, 'Oh God, no doubt they are, I've told them not to often enough, but they're just hungry.' For saying that, I inwardly begged her pardon for some of the wicked things I have thought about her. But of course I know she is not speaking out of any feeling for us but out of hatred, envy and *Schadenfreude* toward the wealthy L. family and especially the battleaxe. She knows full well that both of them were in the same position once, both were servant girls, and she cannot forgive the battle-axe her prosperity while she herself has only worked herself up to being an assistant wardress in a prison. So: five minutes later the battleaxe spotted Mariechen chewing away, her cheeks full. I noticed that she was watching us through the office window, and by-way of provocation I broke myself a large hunk off a fresh roll before her very eyes. She rushed out in a fury. 'Frl. H., Frl. H., two more thefts.' I laughed out loud. 'Right,' she yelled, 'I'm phoning the public prosecutor and you'll be charged with theft.' 'Fine,' I said boldly, 'you do that. But just remember one thing: one day the way you've treated us here will all be paid back.' She gave me a fleeting glance but made no answer. Frl. H., of course, said, 'Keep your mouth shut, R.!' So we have been warned. But we are hard-boiled sinners and it is Saturday, with a long afternoon and a long Sunday ahead of us, and there is no white bread on a Monday morning. We will be hungry for two days. No, we won't go hungry, we shall take some white bread with us, but not in our pockets, we're not that stupid. We know that we will be searched ('frisked' is the technical term). Before we leave the bakery we have to get in line. The battleaxe and Fräulein H. frisk us, that is to say they pat us all over, hunting for pieces of bread. They find nothing. The battleaxe frisks me, or rather she is about to. With a grin, I show her my empty pockets and open my jacket.

She moves on without a word. Frl. H. is more experienced. She pats my back. She says, 'No, you're not like that.' 'No,' I say, 'I'm not like that.' The search produces no result. We have nothing on us. When we get back to the prison we have to report to the office because the battleaxe has phoned the police. There we stand, in front of the governor. 'You've been eating bread again, have you?' We bow our heads, hypocritically confessing our guilt. I say, 'We're so hungry. The others who work outside get bread, sausage, and milk, but what do we get? We just eat a mouthful or so when we're hungry, that's all.' He says, 'I don't know how often I've suggested they should give you each a piece of bread over there, but . . . Anyway, if you do steal, don't take more than you can put into your mouths, and don't do it when you can be seen. Off you go.' In the cell we unpack: B. has a lengthy hunk of bread tied inside each trouser leg, Käthe has some in her scarf, I have some on my head under my headscarf ('I'm not like that'), Mariechen has some in her armpits, Resi in her stockings.

12 December 1944

Sunday. Alarm, all-clear, alarm, all day long. It is snowing. A Christmas atmosphere. We are downcast, tired, hungry, the white bread doesn't last, there was too much salt in our food at lunch and we bolted it too fast, in between the bombing and firing. I am so tired that I don't care at all if a bomb hits me. We have been given books. This time I got Mörike's poems, but I don't care for them. Earlier, I know, I used to love 'O flaumenleichte Zeit der ersten Frühe', or 'Früh wenn die Hähne krähn'. But now it has all fallen mute for me, without music. We lie on our bunks, most of us asleep. Frau H. has had a heart attack and is still groaning as a matter of habit. I look at their faces, these faces with their mouths hanging open, grown grey, slack, and ugly, these emaciated figures in dirty rags. A louse is crawling along Käthe's hair behind her ear, very slowly. Käthe scratches herself in her sleep. Resi has been sitting on the bucket for a good while. There is quite a stench. I got up on the bed and opened the window a little. The air is fresh and cold. It is snowing. I hate these creatures in here. I can't stand them any more. And still the end of the war is not in sight. The sirens are sounding yet again.

13 December 1944

A little change in the eternal round. Today the owner himself came to the bakery, a short, fat, very good-looking man. He gazed at us prisoners. For a moment, without meaning it, I tried to look prettier, and in a fit of coquettishness gave him a smile. He said hello. He needed four prisoners to help with rearrangements in his warehouse. Frl. H. picked Odette, Resi I (the farmgirl) and Resi II (the deserter's lover), and me. We put on our jackets and went along. We walked halfway across the town. I had not seen the town since my childhood. It is a small place, and has not been bombed yet, but is melancholy nevertheless. The display windows are empty, the road surfaces are in need of repair, the houses are dark with age and rain and want repairing everywhere. The people we encounter are melancholy too, harassed, ill-tempered. They shove us aside, uncouthly and hastily, and stare at us with curiosity and contempt. Someone asked, 'Are they Poles or Ukrainians or what?' A grumpy woman answered, 'No, they're gaolbirds, thieves or something like that.' We have L.G.T. stamped on our jackets and skirts (Landgerichtsgefängnis Traunstein).* We went to a spacious storehouse where we had to shift an endless quantity of huge stacks of folded cardboard boxes. It was fairly hard work, and the storehouse was ice-cold and draughty. Herr L. worked with us, puffing, in shirtsleeves and braces, his fat watch-chain across his full belly. Plainly the work needed to be done in a hurry. We talked. I found it pleasant to be talking to a man for once. L. is one of those bourgeois who, with some effort, conceal their financial greed, their quaking fear of losing their money and their other possessions, and their gluttony and lust beneath a man-of-the-world veneer. I noticed him making eyes at pretty Odette. He speaks French. Odette's reply was all one could wish. Every movement of hers is so full of natural coquetry that a man such as L. has to fall for her. In reality she was amused at his expense, pointed to his fat backside when his back was turned, and aped him. He asked why I was in prison. I told him. He cracked a few jokes about Hitler and the Nazis and told me he knew Eva Braun, Hitler's mistress. He put on an anti-Nazi act, and I'd have enjoyed speaking my loathing with him too if some instinct hadn't warned me against him. At ten he went to fetch sausage and bread for us. He locked us in. For a quarter of an hour we were on our own. It was a wonderful, illuminating quarter-hour. Naturally we did not go on working but instead looked round the warehouse. We found a pile of packages that felt soft; the pile was about a metre and a half high, and just as broad and deep. We tore one corner open and discovered

* i.e. Traunstein District Prison. (Translator)

bales of cloth, suit materials, overcoat materials, marvellous woollens. Furthermore: in a dark corner of the warehouse, some sixty sacks of sugar, hundreds of sacks of white flour, crates of almonds, nuts, raisins. Unfortunately we could only hear the nuts rattling, only smell the raisins.—The crates were securely nailed up. There were also about fifty or sixty boxes that smelt of vanilla. The boxes were fastened with wire and couldn't be opened. On an impulse, Odette ripped open a corner, and vanilla sugar sifted out. Hastily and greedily we started licking, but we were unable to get much that way. Odette had a good idea: all of us always have our spoons in our pockets. So we ate the sugar with our spoons. It burnt our throats but it was sweet. Then Odette rustled up little bags which we filled with the sugar. We stuffed our knickers and blouses full of them. But then we suddenly noticed that the whole storehouse was fragrant with the scent of vanilla. What were we to do? We heard the keys jangling. L. was coming back. Turmoil. L. didn't bring us rolls but instead rye bread and a poor-quality, cheap wurst. But still, wurst is wurst, and in spite of the vanilla sugar we were hungry. At length L. sniffed at the air. I got in first, and said, 'Herr L., did you know a box of vanilla sugar's torn? We were going to lift it down and saw the corner was off it. Must be mice.' He said, 'Ach, these damned mice. They really eat everything. I shall have to put out mousetraps.' He climbed back to the boxes right away – and the god of thieves was merciful to us, there were mouse droppings on the floor. We were saved. Vanilla sugar was scattered on the floor. He said, 'Sweep this up and throw it away.' I stared at him. Did it really not occur to him to say, 'You have it'? Does he really not know what an exquisite luxury sugar is for us? No – God knows, he has no idea. He's got everything he needs. He doesn't know that there are people who are starving.—I also realised what the warehouse rearrangements meant. When we returned in the afternoon the bales of material and the sacks of sugar had been removed. I asked innocently, 'What's become of the bales that were there?' He said, 'Oh, that's just sackcloth for the flour-sacks. We've put them where they'll be safe from bombs. You never know.' 'True,' I said, 'you're quite right there, Herr L., you never can tell. Good job if you've provided for leaner times. I say you should eat your fill as long as you're able.' He glanced at me distrustingly. I laughed: 'Herr L., if I were in your position I wouldn't be so afraid of the bombs, I'd be more afraid of times to come when you can't have as much as you like while others have nothing.' I gave him a friendly smile. He cleared his throat and went. He won't want me there again. Nor do I need to go back, I saw quite enough. In the evening Frau R. told me that L. has already brought charges against three prisoners he'd tempted into saying things against Hitler.

14 December 1944

Another chapter in the story of L.: today at the bakery Christmas biscuits were being baked for the L. family all day long. For hours the fragrance was in our noses. The four super-blonde girls flitted busily to and fro carrying plates of baked biscuits right past us to the office, all kinds of things I hadn't seen or eaten for years, peacetime biscuits yellow from the eggs and smelling of butter, sprinkled with coloured sugar, decked with hazelnuts and almonds, topped with thick chocolate coating, smelling of rum or arrack. In the afternoon, as usual, we could also

141

smell real coffee and cigarettes. L. turned up himself, with his son, and they ate and drank for hours. When one of our machines developed a minor fault, Mariechen had to fetch the battleaxe from the office. Mariechen told us there were two big liqueur bottles on the table, and a whole lot of biscuits on the floor by the dog basket. The dog had plainly eaten too much. She had swiftly stolen a few cigarette butts that were also on the floor. When the wardress was outside for a short while we stood on chairs and stared in through the office window. We were within an ace of rebellion, but the wardress came back and we raced to our places. As of that moment we represented a united front of hatred. We didn't say a word; but five minutes later the broad leather belt on Odette's machine tore. The battleaxe had to take it off and put it in for repair. Machine number I thus had nothing to do, so she stuffed herself unreservedly with white bread. The wardress looked away. Another five minutes had passed when a spring shot out of my machine and vanished without trace. It took ten minutes till the battleaxe had fitted a replacement. Then suddenly the funnel of the filling machine was clogged and couldn't be freed. Then my belt tore too (I had unpicked the seam), and machine number II was inoperative too. The battleaxe carried out the repairs in silence. Scarcely were the two belts back in working order but there was a short circuit. We had been running the machines too fast. While we were at it we filled old rags and scraps of paper into the bags instead of breadcrumbs, sealed them as prescribed, and packed them into the boxes. They were loaded up in the evening and will be dispatched tomorrow. Käthe caught one or two cockroaches, these revolting brown beetles that creep about the bakery in their hundreds, and packed those too.

Then suddenly the heating packed in. It was desperate. When the cable on the boxing machine snapped as well, the battleaxe began to swear. 'Ach,' I said *sotto voce*, 'why get excited? Soon it won't be possible to transport anything anyway, nearly all the railways have been bombed.' Frau R. said, 'Come, come, you know the Führer will have some way of seeing that an essential war effort like the production of breadcrumbs gets along all right.' The battleaxe didn't give us so much as a glance. We crammed as much white bread into our mouths as we could. We crunched it loudly, right beside the battleaxe, but she didn't say a word. Perhaps she had got the message.

In the evening, instead of 360 we had packed only 220 boxes.

15 December 1944

A further chapter in the tale of L.: today some farmwomen came in from the country with big baskets. In the afternoon, the dog and cat were let out of the office of a sudden, and one of the blonde girls tossed something bloody onto the floor by our machines. It was the head and craw of a goose. The dog and cat ate it choosily. We stared, mutely. During our break we saw that the hens in the courtyard had had a mountain of wheat scattered for them.

Why do these people do such things in front of our eyes? Is it thoughtlessness? There are people who have never in all their lives suffered hunger or even the slightest need. Their ability to have compassion with others has atrophied.—Probably they consider us prisoners stupid and no risk into the bargain. We don't see a thing! And if we did see anything, what could we do about it? And indeed, it's true: we could do nothing. We have to content ourselves with sabotaging belts, losing screws, and straining springs. The number of boxes we packed today sank to two hundred. Frl. H. registers nothing, deliberately. The battleaxe rants within careful limits, but inside she is boiling with rage. Today I offered the dog and cat the crust of my breakfast rye bread. They gobbled it eagerly. They won't take white bread. Black bread is a delicacy for them. Sausage skins lie around uneaten. This evening Käthe prayed: 'Dear God, have ten bombs fall on L.'s bakery and five on L.'s house, or else I won't believe in you any more.'

16 December 1944

My lawyer has been. He has applied for a twelve-day interruption in my term, to enable me to spend Christmas at home. He thinks it may be approved but feels I should not raise my hopes. I don't, any more. At all. I told him the 'midwife' with her abortion count had been released. He shrugged his shoulders. 'You know,' he said in his rhetorical way, 'I am a man trying to cry out in a dream and unable to do so. I am unhappier than you.' To that I said nothing.

17 December 1944

The big political sensation is that [Field-Marshal] Runstedt has launched a counter-offensive on the Rhine. The Americans are retreating. Germany is triumphing, and so are many of the prisoners. 'Now we will win the war.' I say, 'Stupid crew, idiots. At best it's a last attempt before the total collapse.' Apart from Frau R., and the woman from Bremen, nobody believes me. Frau H., the one-time Austrian 'illegal', is beaming: 'Our Führer! Didn't I always say it: he'll let the enemy come right to the border, into the trap, and then hammer them.' Frau Sch. says, 'Cow.'

What is to become of Germany if the Nazis win? But they won't win, I know they won't. Still, I am in despair.

20 December 1944

The Germans are still advancing. Whatever is the matter with the Americans? Are they having supply problems? Or difficulty with reinforcements? Why are they hesitating? I don't understand a thing any more. The food here is so poor that we can hardly eat a thing any more. Only Z. eats four or five helpings. She scrapes out everyone's leftovers. 'Have to see we don't make the prison a present of anything,' she says, grinning. Today all four of my potatoes were rotten. I complained. The wardress went to the kitchen to fetch me some better ones. She came back without my plate. There were no more left. I yelled, 'What am I supposed to eat, then?' And I threw a few bad potatoes at the wall, where they stuck fast. The others froze. The wardress gave me a warning but then she went. What is she to do about it? It's not her fault.

This afternoon my blister suddenly burst. Thick yellow pus streamed down on the breadcrumbs and the machine. The wound was quickly bandaged and I had to go on working. The bandage was soaked in blood in a moment, and the packets I have handled today all have traces of blood and pus on them. So what? None of it matters.

In our cell this evening we played an old prisoners' game to cheer me up. (For the first time I was in need of comfort, though no one would believe it.) First they threw a shoe. Then, from where the shoe landed, they placed one shoe after another, heel to toe, from each of us, making a line of touching shoes from the one that was first thrown to the cell door. They say that the one whose shoe ends up closest to the door this way will be the first to be released. My shoe was nearest the door. No doubt they fixed it that way to comfort me. I flung the shoes into a corner and bawled. They sat round me helplessly, with no notion what they should do. I shouted: 'That's what your Führer has done for you, all of it, this filth, being hungry, being miserable. That lunatic, that crook.' They put their hands on my mouth. But it's all one to me. Now I am calm again. There is a wooden board by my head: they hit me on the head for my own good. Now I am numbed.

21 December 1944

Today some of the prisoners were suddenly released, including all those who had affairs with foreigners. Why? Has our counter-attack been thrown back? The prison is throbbing with excitement. Everyone is waiting to be set free. Me too. Late in the evening my lawyer came and had me summoned. I rushed in to him. Nothing. He said the application had been turned down, otherwise I'd have been released today along with the rest.

Fine – let us celebrate Christmas in prison, then. My Christmas parcel has already arrived. A book from K., from Ma a cake, and biscuits, apples, nuts, a sprig of fir with a candle. I had opened it at midday and by evening half the biscuits and apples had already been stolen. Ach, I don't care about anything. Anything at all.

Roughly ten minutes later. Today they are leaving the lights on a long time. In these last few minutes I have come a long way from wild despair and violent fear of death to composure. Why was I really so despairing? Mainly because I was afraid of Christmas Eve. I was thinking of the children. But that is sentimentality. The children will celebrate Christmas without me. A lot of children are having to spend it without a father or mother. And why was I frightened of dying? I haven't been condemned to death yet. And what if I had been. For a moment I felt a deep relief at the thought of death. I believe I shall now be able to bear whatever fate is in store for me.

One year later

On 12 October 1945, exactly one year after I was arrested, I received a letter from the woman whose denunciation led to my being charged. This letter was really written.

A., October 1945

Luise,

You are taking a bitter revenge. Sepp has been under arrest for nine weeks. I do not think he will be coming back. I was given a job initially in a *Volksschule* but have been dismissed again, so I am homeless with three children.

I want to beg your forgiveness. That is all. The consequences are mine to bear. I have learnt painfully enough that you were right. At that time I could not believe the dreadful things you told me, it was too much. In one hour you shattered the image I had had of the world for over ten years and which I had believed good and proper. In my inner need I had to break my promise to keep silence. I wrote; Sepp made the denunciation; I had to testify. It was hard enough for me and I have often regretted it.

Now you are doing what you believe right. Bear in mind that we too did what we believed right, because we could

not see behind the scenes. That is all I have to say. I wish
you only well.

Lisl

This was my reply:

K., 12 October 1945

Lisl,

   You are mistaken if you suppose I am to blame for your
misfortunes. I did not bring any charge against you. Do
you know me so poorly that you could believe I would
want revenge? What I fought was your enthusiasm for war
and for National Socialism. I did it because I abhorred
both, just as I abhor everything that is born of violence
and hatred. How could I now do the very thing I fought
against in you? What you did to me, and what you added
to the great sum of mankind's guilt, will be avenged of
itself according to an unmerciful law. I shall let others take
the opportunity to revenge themselves; I myself shall not
do it because I do not believe that blood can avenge blood.
You offer me your apologies. It is both needless and
senseless to do so. Needless, because for me the sufferings
of prison have long become of no consequence, and far
outweighed by the spiritual gains of that time. Your
apologies are senseless because they come too late and
arise in an unclean source. Your belief in Hitler collapsed
at the very moment that National Socialism collapsed.
What is behind your change of heart is not a perception of
the lying, evil, stupid, and inhuman nature of that regime
but merely the bitter experience that it could not survive.
It does not take much to recognise that something was
wrong after a collapse of that order.

   You say you found it hard enough to have been the

cause of my being charged. Do you remember 1 February, when we saw each other again at that terrible hearing (for me, it lasted eight hours) before the Reich security police in Berchtesgaden? You know that my lawyer had struggled on my behalf to make sure of that confrontation, because we believed you would use the opportunity to retract or at least water down your testimony, on which everything rested. You looked at me full of hatred. Maybe it was insecurity or repentance that hardened you in that way. When I made a statement in my defence you shouted out: 'She's lying.' You knew that your testimony was putting me in extreme danger. You knew that sedition and high treason carried the death penalty, or years in a concentration camp. You knew that I have two small children that would be left without a mother if I were condemned on your testimony. You knew that Sepp made the denunciation because he was afraid that if political sense, and an urgent, unselfish love of peace, became too popular, he would lose his pleasant, comfortable position as an officer at the Allenstein casino. No, I do not accept your apologies. I myself have got over everything that concerned me, even the rupture of the friendship we once had. What I can neither forget nor forgive is the hatred that was in your eyes. That was not you, it was the madness that had seized hold of you, just as it had seized hold of the countless others.

But now let us make an end of hatred, blood, and death. What we want – we who have survived, who have truly learnt something in these terrible years – is peace and humanity.

Luise

151